JACK

A Story of a Young Boy's Faith

JACK CROCKETT

ISBN 978-1-64258-654-1 (paperback)
ISBN 978-1-64258-655-8 (digital)

Christian Faith Publishing, Inc.
832 Park Avenue
Meadville, PA 16335
www.christianfaithpublishing.com

Printed in the United States of America

CHAPTER 1

SUMMERTIME

It's another hot July afternoon, and nine-year-old Jack Andrews has been out in the sun a long time. Earlier today, after lunch, he helped his mother with the flower garden. He took a walk and spent time skipping rocks at a nearby creek. He has just returned to his own backyard. Wiping the sweat from his forehead, he sat down on the soft green grass and then lay on his back. The grass feels cool and smells so good. He brought his pretend binoculars to his face and began to scan the sky. Fluffy big clouds of all shapes are slowly passing overhead. He enjoys the cool shadow they cast on his face. His attention is focused on a cloud as it climbs upward in height. It is shaped like a mountain. Jack watches in awe as it climbs higher and higher in the sky. The sun makes one side bright white, but the other side is dark, almost black. The sight reminds him of Reverend Perrin's Sunday-morning sermon. He told of how God called Moses up on the mountain that had thunder and lightning. Moses spent forty days and nights on the mountain with God and went down carrying the two tablets of stone. On the stones were the commandments of God. Jack wonders, "What does God look like?"

The cloud is moving on, and the sun feels hot on his face. It is time to retreat to his most favorite place. He jumped up and ran around to the front yard. Leaping off the sidewalk, he caught hold of the first big branch and pulled himself up. He sat down, let his legs dangle over the branch, and leaned against the tree's huge trunk. "Ah, it's great." He placed his hands behind his head and closed his eyes. The shade of the tree, with a breeze blowing through the leaves, is so peaceful. "It's like heaven without the angels," Jack whispered to himself.

He can look up through the branches and see the clouds passing overhead. Birds are singing and don't seem to mind sharing the tree with him. He listened as the locusts began their humming. He sighed and smiled. "Yep, just like heaven," he said as he began humming along with them. His humming turned to singing. It's a song he learned in Sunday school, when he was a much-younger boy, but he still loves the tune. He is singing "Zacchaeus was a wee little man and a wee little man was he. He climbed up in a sycamore tree, for the Lord he wanted to see. And the Lord said, 'Zacchaeus, you come down. I'm going to your house today. I'm going to your house to stay.'" Humming another verse, he stopped and wondered, "How did Jesus know Zacchaeus was in the tree? Does Jesus know I'm in this tree?" as he looked upward through the big tree's branches.

"Hello, Jack," a voice said. "Jesus?" Jack responded under his breath, surprised by the voice. "Little Jack, what are you doing?" the voice continued. Through the leaves of the tree, Jack can see a pair of farmers' overalls. It is Mr. Jones. His friendly smile became visible as he leaned toward the tree, pulling the leaves back with his leathery big hands. Mr. Jones is a retired gentleman who lives in the neighborhood. All the neighborhood kids love Mr. Jones, especially Jack. They are good friends. Now in full view and smiling, he said again, "What are you doing, little Jack?"

"Oh, just hanging around," Jack answered as he reached over and picked up a locust sitting on a nearby branch. The locust began to vibrate and hum even louder than before as Jack closed his fingers around it. He pulled his hand close to his face and pretended to be shaving with an electric shaver. Mr. Jones laughed. "Well, have a good time now, and careful you don't fall," he said with a chuckle. "Yes, sir, I will. Bang," Jack said as he fired his six-shooter, releasing the locust, which left his hand like a bullet fired into the air. Mr. Jones laughed again as he began his journey home, down the long sidewalk. Jack watched the white-haired old gentleman disappear around the big elm tree on the corner and said to himself, "Mr. Jones is a nice man."

Wiggling back up against the tree's trunk again, Jack stayed there the rest of the afternoon, humming and singing with his friends in the tree. After a while, he noticed a quiet is beginning to settle over the tree, and the sky through the big branches is taking on a pale gray color. The sun is setting, and the fireflies are beginning their evening dance. Jack has always thought watching their performance was the very best way to end a summer's day. A voice calls, "Jack, time to come in now." It is his mother. "Coming," Jack replied as he bailed from the tree. He ran toward the house, holding his arms stretched out with his hands cupped. "Got one," he said as he came to a stop. The firefly seems pleased to stay on his hand as it walks from finger to finger. It tickles, and Jack laughed quietly. He gently raised his hand in the air, and the insect took its place among the others. He stepped up on the porch, turned, and watched a few moments more. Opening the old screen door, he looked back at his sanctuary, the big tree he loves so much, and he sighed. The day is done. The screen door squeaked, as he entered the house for a night's rest. The fireflies continue to dance as the quiet darkness deepened. The birds and locusts have now become quiet, and the only noise from the tree is from the leaves moving in the gentle summer breeze. The dew is beginning to form on the grass. The moon and the stars are now the rulers of the skies, as the world begins preparing new wonders for a young boy named Jack.

A MATTER OF CONSCIENCE

The last week of July has been a full one. Vacation Bible school at Community Church ended on Friday. It's Saturday, and Jack and two other boys from the neighborhood are busy in the garage. The old bicycle inner tubes, leather strings, and some strong sticks produce what the boys hope for. They each have their own slingshot. The boys' favorite Bible time of the week was the story of David, fighting and defeating the Philistine giant called Goliath. This inspired the idea of making a slingshot. Bobby drew a mean-looking face on a big paper grocery sack. He placed the sack over the straw head of the broom that his younger brother, Ted, has stuck in the ground. There is the giant, Goliath. Jack has been gathering as many small round stones as he can find. He then divided them between himself and the other two boys. "Ready, aim, fire!" yelled Ted. All three boys began shooting the pebbles at the old giant as fast as they could, giggling the whole time. "I need more stones," said Bobby as he reloaded and fired. "Me too!" yelled Ted. Unaware of the pretended battle going on, a sparrow sought to land on the head of Goliath and then suddenly fell to the ground. All three boys stop, stunned at what has happened. Slowly approaching where the bird landed, Jack planted the knees of his jeans on the ground and then carefully picked up the bird. There is no movement, no sign of life. "It was an accident," Ted said. "It's just a bird anyway," said Bobby. "We didn't mean to hit him," he continued. A few moments passed in silence as all three boys watch the lifeless body of the bird in Jack's hands. A sound of music playing from down the street broke the silence. Looking at the direction of the music, Bobby pointed and said with excitement, "It's the ice cream truck. Let's go." Ted and Bobby took off in a run and then stopped. "Come on, Jack," the boys called together, waving with their hands. Jack, still holding the sparrow, shook his head. "Okay," said the boys as they ran out of sight.

Hot tears are running down Jack's cheeks. His throat is growing tight. "I'm so sorry." He can hardly get the words out. He is sick at heart. He loves the birds. He loves their singing and sharing the big tree with them. His tears are making prints on the dry ground as a tall shadow is approaching from behind him. "Are you hurt, little Jack?" The voice is that of Mr. Jones, but Jack can hardly see him for the salty tears in his eyes. "Now, Jack," said Mr. Jones, bending down as he wiped the tears from Jack's eyes with his thumb. "What has happened here?" he asked.

Bowing his head, feeling ashamed, Jack lifted the bird toward Mr. Jones. "We killed him, Mr. Jones. We didn't mean to," he said. "We were just shooting our slingshots, and the bird flew by, and one of our stones hit him. I'm so sorry," he said as tears fell from his eyes. His eye is on the sparrow. "Jack," Mr. Jones said as he got on one knee to talk to him face-to-face. "Huh?" said Jack as he wiped his face with the back of his hand. "Well, Jack," Mr. Jones started. "Jesus said, not one sparrow falls to the ground without your heavenly Father. You see, Jack, even this little bird didn't die alone, without someone caring. As this little fellow fell from the sky, God himself was with him. God saw and knows it was an accident, Jack." A moment passed, and Jack answered, "I still feel awful."

"Yes, I know, life's lessons are sometimes difficult," replied the old gentleman. He gently pulled Jack's chin upward so that their eyes met and said," "Jesus said something else, Jack, something about you and me."

"Really?" Jack asked. Mr. Jones answered, "Jesus said, 'Are you not of greater value than many sparrows?' Jack, always remember that God loves you and is always there to help you and to save you." Jack managed a tiny smile. He does feel somewhat better even though he doesn't understand why.

Standing up and taking Jack by the hand, Mr. Jones said, "We have one thing left to do." The old gentleman led Jack to the big tree that he loves so much. Taking a pocketknife from his overalls, he dug a small grave on the side of the tree that gets the morning sun. He took the bird from Jack, placed it in the hole, and gently covered it with the dirt. Then he took out his handkerchief and dried Jack's eyes. He patted him gently on the head and said, "Remember, Jack, God always knows, and he always loves us." Jack nodded and smiled.

Mr. Jones said goodbye, and Jack crawled up in the tree. He stayed there for the rest of the day, quiet, listening to the birds singing, as he looked up through the tree's big branches. He is feeling better and is glad his good friend Mr. Jones was there to help. The hours have passed, and Jack is tired. The sun is beginning to set. The birds are growing quiet as they find a place to perch for the night. The old screen door opened with its familiar screech. "Jack, time to come in, Sunday school tomorrow," his mother said. "Yes, Mother," he replied. "Don't forget to take out the trash," she added. Jack waved, nodded, and hopped out of the tree. He emptied the trash into the big can in the backyard and stood there for a short while. Then he turned, and looked at the big tree out front and walked to the house. He stepped inside and let the door close, slowly, with hardly a sound. A few minutes later, the sun is no longer visible. The cool evening breeze is beginning to blow. The fireflies are dancing, as stars twinkle high above. All is quiet. The moon's soft rays are reaching toward the earth, revealing the evidence of a decision that a young boy made; as a matter of conscience. There on the top of the trash can is Jack's slingshot.

SOMEBODY'S PRAYING

It is a warm Sunday-morning walk to the Community Church building. Jack has taken his usual route from his home, down to the corner, and through an alleyway. It is a grassy area. The back fence of each house on the street is on either side. Jack stopped as he reached the last fence on the right. He listened. She is there. He can hear her breathing. Looking through the space between the boards of the fence, he can see two brown eyes looking at him. "Ready, set, go!" Jack yelled as he ran. He stopped quickly at the other end of the fence. She is already there, just seconds before him, with her paws hanging over the fence. "Well, you win again," Jack said as he patted Shasta on the head. Shasta is Mr. Jones's beautiful German shepherd. Jack leaned toward the fence, and Shasta licked him on his right cheek. In his whole life, he has never won a race against Shasta. "Bye, girl," he said as he looked both ways and crossed the street.

The sidewalks and parking lot around the church building are busy as people arrive for the Sunday school hour. Bobby, Ted, and many of the other kids from Jack's class have gathered at the side door. Seeing Jack, Bobby yelled, "Hey, Jack, come on." Jack ran to the door, and they all entered together. It is a beautiful building with tall walls and stained-glass windows. Their classroom is just down the hall, two doors from the water fountain. A lot of the kids are still excited and talking about the Vacation Bible School, which ended on Friday. The big hallway echoes their joy. As the last door closed shut, the hallway became quiet, as the hour of Bible study, and prayer began. Jack looks forward to going to church. His neighborhood playmates are in his class, and his mother and father are just down the hall. He loves hearing of the works of God in the lives of people told of in the Bible. He especially loves the colorful big pictures his Sunday-school teacher has on the walls, as she teaches of God from the holy scriptures, as she calls them.

An hour has passed, and the bell to end Sunday school is ringing. The organ in the big sanctuary has already begun to play as the classroom doors swing open. The hallways are busy once again as members of the congregation greet one another. Jack stopped at the water fountain. As he began to sip, he heard a voice say, "Hi, Jack." He looked up as he wiped the water from his chin. It's Von Martin. Her bright blue eyes always seemed to sparkle when she smiled, and naturally, Jack smiled back. He hasn't been able to explain it to himself, but Von's smile gives him a warm feeling inside. He always welcomes her presence. Von is ten years old, the older sister of Bobby and Ted. "Mother made brownies last night, Jack. Want to come over after lunch?" Von asked hurriedly. Jack smiled even bigger and nodded. "Good, see you later," she said, still smiling. She hugged her little red Bible to her chest and hurried through the big wooden doors that lead into the sanctuary. Jack tucked his little black Bible under his arm and went through the big doors and down the long hallway. He sat down on the small pew in the back, at the right-hand corner of the sanctuary. He looked up at the lighted exit sign over the door just a few steps away and smiled again. Von's mother makes the best brownies in the neighborhood.

The adult choir called everyone to worship as they began singing "Holy, Holy." The choir led in many of the familiar old songs. Reverend Perrin then stood and asked everyone to turn to the text in the Bible that he would be addressing in his sermon. Jack turned to the sixth chapter of Matthew and listened. Once Reverend Perrin got started, he could get "a little long-winded," as Jack's father has often said. It's hard for young boys to sit still very long, but Jack knew he had to try. After a while, his mind began to wander from the sermon. He can see his good friend Mr. Jones sitting in his usual place, and beside him is Mrs. Jones, who is wearing a new blue hat. Reverend Perrin raised his voice, making a point, as he often does. In response,

Jack quickly turned his attention forward, and something caught his eye. It is the big stained-glass window, on the tall wall, behind the pulpit.

The sun's rays make the figures on the windows seem to come alive. Jack knew the windows were there, but somehow, it all seems different. There are two men on the window. One man is rugged looking, with a heavy beard, wearing an animal skin for clothes. The other man Jack recognizes from pictures in his Bible. It is Jesus. Both men are standing in a river, and the rugged man is pouring water on Jesus's head. The thing that catches Jack's attention the most is a bird. It is beautiful, with its wings spread. It is landing on Jesus. *How strange,* he thought to himself. He is captivated by the sight. He is strangely moved, as he continues looking at the window. *What does it all mean?* he wondered. His thoughts are interrupted, and the sight of the window is blocked, as the man in front of him stands with the congregation for prayer. When the closing prayer was over, Jack was out the door and on his way home. *I'll ask Dad about the windows at lunch,* he thought. He crossed the street, met Shasta for the return race, and lost, as usual. Patting the winner on the head, he smiled, and Shasta answered with a quick bark. Giggling, Jack was again on the trail home to have lunch with his mother and father.

Mr. Andrews has just said "Amen," ending his prayer of thanks for the hot meal on the table before the family. "Amen," said Jack as he pulled a chicken leg from the big platter and onto his plate. After all the side dishes had been passed among the family of three, they began to enjoy the blessings on the table. Jack can't help but notice how peaceful and secure it all seems to be. "Great meal, Mother," Mr. Andrews said. Jack, taking a big bite of his chicken leg, nodded and smiled as he chewed. "Thank you, boys," said Mrs. Andrews, winking at Jack. "How was Sunday school, Jack?" she asked. He took a quick drink of his milk, swallowed, and said, "It was great."

"Hey, Dad," he continued, "can I ask you a question?"

"Why of course," Mr. Andrews replied, placing his fork on the table. He leaned slightly forward, as if to assure Jack of his undivided attention. Jack started his questions. "Well, the big windows behind

Reverend Perrin, do they tell a story? I mean, who is the man with the beard, and what does the bird mean?"

His father began his explanation. "The man with the beard is John the Baptist, the prophet God sent to prepare the people, for Jesus's coming. God told him, he would recognize the Christ. While John was baptizing, Jesus came forward and asked him to baptize him. As John was baptizing Jesus, the spirit of God descended from heaven in the form of a dove and lighted upon Jesus. By this, John understood that God had fulfilled his promise and the Christ was Jesus. Do you understand, Jack?" his father asked. "Well, sort of," Jack replied. Then he asked, "Dad, why are people baptized?" His father answered, "Jesus told Peter, James, and John and the other apostles to preach the good news of God's forgiveness of our sins. He also told them, those who believed should be baptized in the name of the Father, the Son, and the Holy Spirit. You see, Jack, baptism is the way people show they are receiving Jesus and are dedicating their lives to following him." Mr. Andrews smiled and asked, "Do you understand, son?"

"I think so," Jack answered. His father said, "Whenever you have questions, son, you can always ask me. Your mother and I want you to understand the things of God."

"I will, thanks, Dad," he said as he began to finish his lunch as fast as he could. "Great lunch, Mom, may I go to Von's?" he asked as he rose from his chair. "Home before dark," his mother said. Jack kissed her on the cheek and ran out the door. The slap of the old screen door caused both Mr. and Mrs. Andrews to laugh with delight in their son.

Only a few minutes' walk, and Jack is in front of Von's home. She is sitting on the porch swing, enjoying the shade. Her blond curls are bouncing in the summer breeze. Looking over her shoulder and seeing Jack, she put her foot down, stopping the swing, and bailed from it in one motion. With an excited smile and her blue eyes gleaming in the bright sun, she said, "Hi, Jack, let's sit on the swing." They sat down, and between them was a basket of brownies. Von served Jack, and then herself. They both lean back onto the old swing, taking bites of the brownies. Each has one foot on the porch floor, making the swing go back and forth as they enjoy the basket of treats. They giggled, sang, and talked until the basket was empty. Rubbing their tummies, they looked at each other and laughed. "What would you like to do now, Jack?" Von asked. "Let's walk down the back path," he answered. Von smiled and nodded. The back path is a large area of unused property where all sorts of flowers grow wild. It also has a winding narrow creek, with tall, slender trees. Jack knows butterflies are often found playing there among the flowers on clear summer days. He hopes they will see some, because he knows Von loves them.

They walked down along the side of the creek. The breeze under the shade of the tall, thin trees is refreshing. Von placed her hand on Jack's shoulder, and he stopped. "Look," Von whispered as she pointed with her other hand. It is a beautiful sight. More butterflies than you can count. Big ones and small ones, of all colors, are fluttering from flower to flower. Quietly and slowly they walked together into the midst of the display. Jack smiled as he watched Von. She stood still as butterflies landed upon her hair and each hand. She giggled softly as one danced on her nose. "I'm so glad God made butterflies," she said. As Von lifted her hands high above her head, the butterflies floated upward from her, as though she were telling them it was time to leave.

Von and Jack started back down the trail, alongside the creek, and up the small hill toward her home, when Von turned and said, "I've been praying for you, Jack." Surprised, Jack looked at her and said, "Really? Why?" Von could tell the boy was puzzled. "Bobby and Ted told me about the bird and how upset you were," she explained. "Oh," he replied as he looked down at the ground and dug the toe of his shoe in the grass. Von responded, "We are supposed to pray for people when they are hurting, Jack." Looking up, he said, "We are?"

"Sure," she replied. "Mother said that there is always someone somewhere praying for you, and when you know someone is hurting, you should always pray for them."

"I didn't know that," he said as he looked at Von. "It's true," she said as she took him by the arm and said, "Come on." They walked back up to the swing and kept it going until it was time for Jack to return home. On his walk home, the air is beginning to cool as the hot August sun lowers on the horizon. In the shade of the trees that line the sidewalk, the fireflies are visible. Jack sighed, "It's been a good day."

The old screen door slammed shut, and Jack's mother and father knew he had arrived safely. "Have a good time, son?" his father asked. "You bet," Jack replied. "I'm glad, son," Mr. Andrews replied. "We best get ready for bed," his mother said from the other room. "Yes, Mother," Jack answered as he headed for his bedroom. Getting things ready quickly, he lay down on his soft bed and looked up at the shadows the moonlight from his window cast on the ceiling. His thoughts are going over the events of the day. "It was a good day," he said to himself quietly. Feeling thirsty, he got up and went to the kitchen for a glass of water. Leaving the kitchen and turning down the hallway, he heard a voice. He paused a moment. He heard his name. He can hear his mother's voice then his father's. He can hear their words. It is true, just as Von said. There is always someone praying for you. Jack quietly walked to his bed, and after a few minutes of thought, he fell asleep. There will be many more days to come that will eventually teach Jack what it is like for a person to kneel before the God of heaven and ask his help for another human being. His growing years will also teach him the meaning of Jesus's words, "Ask, and you shall receive. Seek and you shall find. Knock, and the door shall be opened unto you, for he that asks receives, he that seeks finds, and to him that knocks the door shall be open."

CHAPTER  4

A New Friend

It's now the middle of August, and some of the neighborhood kids are talking about school starting again. Jack is taking a break from the sun's heat by spending time in the shade of the tree he loves so much. The thought of a new school year doesn't excite Jack, because he knows it means the close of the summer and the end of so many things that he loves about the season. He loves school, his friends, and his teachers, but right now, he wants to make the most of his favorite time of year. The wind is blowing gently through the tree's branches, and Jack has kicked back and is taking it all in. His eyes are closed as he tries to identify the different sounds around him. He can hear skate wheels on the pavement just up the street. *Jimmy Pierce*, he thought to himself. The birds in the tree are softly chattering, but he can distinctly hear a mockingbird at the top of the tree. Someone around the corner is mowing the lawn. He can hear the motor running, and he smells the fresh cut grass carried by the wind. A single locust is humming as it sits on a branch just by his left arm. He loves the time alone. A new sound is added as he listens. It is coming closer, and then it stopped just under the tree. Unable to identify it, he opened his eyes and looked down through the tree branches.

There is a man standing on the sidewalk just below the tree, wearing a brown hat, and he has a white wooden cane in his right hand. As Jack looked down at him, the man said, "Hello, young man," but he isn't looking up in the tree where Jack is sitting. Wondering how the man knew he was in the tree, he answered, "Hello, sir." The man then asked if Jack might help him. Jack said "Yes, sir" and climbed out of the tree and stood in front of the stranger. He noticed right away that the man is wearing dark sunglasses. The man smiled, offered his hand, and said, "My name is Clay Sanders." Jack reached forward and smiled as he shook hands with Mr. Sanders. He smiled because shaking hands with someone is something he has never done before. He likes the way it makes him feel. He answered, "My name is Jack Andrews."

"I'm very glad to meet you, Jack," Mr. Sanders replied. He explained to Jack that he has bought the brown house down the street and, while the moving men are getting things inside, he wanted to get to know the neighborhood. He asked Jack to come out of the tree, hoping he could tell him how to get to Community Church. He explained he is planning to attend worship there on Sunday. Jack smiled and told Mr. Sanders that he, his mother, and his father also go to Community Church and that Jack would take him there.

Jack told Mr. Sanders the way to the church as they walked along together. He noticed that Mr. Sanders only looks forward and taps his cane on the sidewalk as they walk along. Mr. Sanders asked if there were any streets to cross. "Only one at the corner," Jack answered. "Once we cross the street, we are in front of the church building." Mr. Sanders asked if Jack would tell him just before they approach the curb of the street they had to cross. "Yes, sir," Jack replied, trying to understand the request. Approaching the curb, Jack said, "The street is just ahead of you, sir."

"Thank you, Jack," Mr. Sanders said, as he took his cane and reached in front of himself, tapping the concrete. "Ah, I got it," Mr. Sanders said. He asked Jack to lead on when he thought it was safe to cross the street. Jack announced the all-clear, and they crossed and stood in front of the church. Mr. Sanders asked if there was a bench in the yard where they may sit down. "Sure," Jack answered, "just over by the front doorway." They walked to the bench just off to the left of the big, tall doors with their beautiful arched top and sat down. "So, Jack, you are what, nine years old?" Mr. Sanders asked. With a proud smile, Jack answered, "Ten, well, in two weeks." He thanked Jack for taking him to the church and said, "It has the feel of a fine place."

"It is," Jack answered.

Mr. Sanders removed his hat, laid his cane against the end of the bench, and said, "I must share a few things with you, Jack, since we are friends now." Jack smiled. He liked it that Mr. Sanders called him a friend. Mr. Sanders then said, "But first I would like to ask you to call me Clay." Jack smiled and nodded. "You bet," he said. Clay laughed. Clay then began an important conversation with his new friend. He said, "Jack, have you wondered about some things being a little strange since we met at the tree?" Jack looked up at Clay, who is smiling at him, and answered, "I wondered why you wanted me to warn you about the curb and why you use the cane to feel the concrete so much."

"That's a very good observation for a boy your age," Clay responded. He explained that he has been blind for several years and that he uses the cane to feel things in front and on either side of him to avoid falls. Jack is surprised. He looked down and then back up at Clay and said, "Clay, if you can't see, how did you know I was in the tree?" Clay chuckled and said, smiling, "Well, that is the other way I have of getting around safely. I heard you move in the tree, so I stopped to listen. I have to admit, I took a chance when I said 'Hello, young man.' I could have been wrong." Jack laughed and said, "I'm glad you stopped." He looked up at Clay and said, "I was in the tree with my eyes closed, trying to imagine where all the different sounds were coming from. I moved in the tree, when I heard your cane on the sidewalk." Clay smiled, patted Jack on the back, and said, "Jack Andrews, I think we are going to be good friends."

"Come on," Clay said as he stood up. "You've got to get me back across that street." The trip back seemed too short for Jack. The time had passed too quickly as he told Clay about Shasta, Mr. Jones, Von, and other things about the neighborhood. Just a little farther, and they will be back where they first met.

There is a man leaning against the trunk of Jack's favorite tree. A few moments of walking reveal that the man is Jack's father. "Hi, Dad," Jack said excitedly as he sprinted the last little distance and hugged his father. Mr. Andrews bent down and hugged him tight. The tapping of Clay's cane stopped as he stood next to father and son. "Well, Clay, I see you found him all right," said Mr. Andrews. "That I did," replied Clay. Mr. Andrews explained to Jack that he and Clay have been friends a long time. He had suggested to Clay that Jack could show him the way to the church. He wanted Jack to meet Clay. Clay and Mr. Andrews then shook hands. Clay thanked Jack again and started his way home, tapping his cane on the sidewalk. "Time to go in, son," said Mr. Andrews as he placed his hand on Jack's shoulder. Jack paused a moment and said, "Dad, can I ask you something?"

"Of course, son, what is it?" he replied. Jack asked, "Did you tell Clay I was in the tree?" Mr. Andrews knelt on one knee so he could look his son in the eye. Then he said with a smile, "I told him he would find you in the tree, but I didn't tell him which tree." They laugh together. Jack understood what his father was saying. Clay had found him by the sounds he made as he moved in the tree. He thought Clay must be a very special person, and he is looking forward to more times with him. The Andrews family is happy that the neighborhood has grown a little and that Clay is its newest member. Jack didn't realize it at the time, but his life is also growing, one friend at a time.

WALK BY FAITH

It's been two days since Jack met Clay at the tree. He has already told Von about their first meeting, and she is looking forward to meeting him at church on Sunday. It's now noon on Saturday, and Jack has been waiting to meet Clay at the tree again. Clay had telephoned Jack's mother earlier and asked if Jack might be able to show him the way downtown. Hearing Clay's cane on the sidewalk, Jack waited until he stopped under the tree. "I know you are up there, Jack," Clay said as he looked upward. "You heard that twig snap, didn't you?" Jack said with a giggle as he lowered himself to the ground. "Yep," Clay replied. 'The twig gave you away for sure." Jack stood in front of Clay. Clay offered his hand, Jack smiled, and the two friends shook hands. "I appreciate you showing me around the town square today, Jack," Clay said. "Oh sure," Jack replied. "What are we going to do downtown?" he asked with a curious look.

"We are going to make a road map," Clay answered. "A road map?" Jack asked, a little surprised. "Well, we need to finish it," Clay replied with a smile. He knew his friend didn't understand. "When did we start it?" Jack asked. Clay explained. "The day you walked me to the church was the beginning of making the map."

"Where is the map?" Jack asked, even more puzzled. "It's in my mind's eye," he replied. Jack stood silent, and Clay put his hand on his shoulder and began to explain. "I counted the number of steps I took from my front sidewalk to here at the tree where I first met you. Then I counted the steps to the curb, and then across the street, and from there, to the bench in front of the church doors," he finished.

"Wow," Jack replied, "I would have never thought of that." Clay went on to explain that, if someone walks him to a place, he simply counts the number of steps and turns and objects, like trees or buildings, along the way. This helps him create a picture in his mind. "I make a map that I read by memory," he said as he looked down at Jack and smiled. Then he added, "It starts with a good friend like you. Are you ready?" he asked. Jack replied with excitement, "You bet, let's go."

So off they went, past Clay's house, to the end of the sidewalk, then a right turn, and walked some more. Jack said, "Just a little farther, and we are at the town square." They walked a few more minutes, and Clay stopped. Then he said, "We are near a building, aren't we?" Jack answered. "We are at the side of Young's Grocery." Clay slowly stepped sideways to his right and extended his hand until he could feel the red brick wall. "Okay, let's continue." He nodded at Jack. Clay kept his hand on the wall as he walked around the corner to the front of the building. Stopping, he said, "We are under the porch roof."

"But how did you know?" Jack asked. Clay explained, "I felt the heat coming from the brick wall, and when we came under the porch, I could tell we were out of the sunshine. It felt cooler."

"That's amazing," Jack said with wonder. "Well, it takes practice," Clay replied, then added, "But it doesn't work when it's snowing." Jack asked, "How do you do it in the snow?" Clay replied with a chuckle, "Still trying to figure that out. Lead the way, my friend."

The two friends walked, and stopped at each building and place of business. Jack introduced Clay to the shop owners. Clay met Mr. Young, the grocer; Mr. Martinez, of the dry cleaners; and Mrs. White, from the post office. As they approached the last building on the square, Clay stopped and sniffed the air. "Something wrong, Clay?" Jack asked, a little concerned. "Nothing wrong with candy," he said as he pointed at the big window in front of them. "Let's go in." Mr. Bailey greeted them with a smile, saying hello to Jack, and then introducing himself to Clay. "What will it be, gentlemen?" he asked with a smile. "Give Jack whatever he wants," Clay replied. "For myself, I'll have the peanut butter fudge." Jack got a small sack of chocolate-covered peanuts. "That's $2.10," Mr. Bailey said. Then Jack saw something that gave him even more admiration for his friend. Clay reached into his pocket, pulled out a handful of coins, and began counting them out to Mr. Bailey. "There you are, Mr. Bailey, and thank you very much," he said with a smile. "Come back soon," said Mr. Bailey as he waved goodbye. The little bell at the top of the door rang as they left the candy shop and closed the door behind them.

"Well, Jack, we best head home. Are you ready?"

"Yes, sir," he said with a mouth full of the chocolate peanuts. As they walked, Jack asked, "Clay, how did you know to give Mr. Bailey the right amount of money?" Folding his empty paper sack and placing it in his pocket, he said, "The coins are different sizes. The smallest is the dime, followed by the penny, the nickel, the quarter, and the half dollar." Jack answered, amazed, "So you felt the size of each coin as you counted the money."

"That's right," Clay replied. "I think you are the smartest person I know," Jack said. Clay patted him on the shoulder and said, smiling, "We never stop learning, Jack. There is always more to learn." Then he continued, "Knowledge is a wonderful thing, but faith is even more important."

"How come?" Jack asked. Clay began, "Truth is like light. By it, we see why, how, and when to do things, but faith is trust in God, and faith gives us the power and courage to do the things we know we must do."

"I'm not sure I understand," Jack said. Clay continued to explain, "When I learned I was blind, I was afraid, because I didn't know what to do. I had depended on my eyes to direct my life. One day, a friend came to see me and told me something Jesus said."

"What did he say?" Jack asked. "He said, 'I am the light of the world. If any man follow me, he shall not walk in darkness, but shall have the light of life.' So I began to trust in him. I can listen to things around me, and I can see things that way. I can count my steps and make a map of town in my mind and go where I want and when I want." Then he finished, "But I must believe God loves me and will lead me, if I'm going to do those things, and not be afraid. Do you understand what I mean, Jack?"

Jack spoke up, excited. "Sure, Mr. Jones once told me his eye is on the sparrow. He said it was something that Jesus said, to teach us that God loves us. He was helping me with a problem that day." "I would sure like to hear that story, if you want to tell me," Clay added. "You bet," Jack said with confidence. He began telling his new friend of the events of the sparrow and the slingshots. He hasn't told anyone about it since it happened. The rest of the walk home was just enough time for Jack to tell what happened that day, and they were in front of the tree where they started. "That's a good story, Jack," Clay said. "I'm glad Mr. Jones was there to help you."

"Me too," he replied. "He is a good friend."

"So are you, Jack," Clay answered as he reached to shake hands. "See you tomorrow," he said as he turned and began his walk home. "Goodbye," Jack said as he smiled and waved his hand. Then he called out "Clay, how many steps did we go today?" Clay stopped, turned, and replied with a smile, "942."

"Wow," Jack whispered to himself.

He watched a few moments as Clay continued down the sidewalk, and then he ran to the front porch. The screen door screeched, as he opened it, stuck his head in, and shouted, "Mom, I'm home! I'll be outside."

"Okay, son," she shouted back from the kitchen. Jack let the screen door slap shut as he ran toward the big tree. He leaped up, grabbed a limb, and made his way to his favorite seat. He leaned back against the tree's big trunk and took a deep breath. The tree smells so good in the late afternoon's cooler air. He closed his eyes and concentrated on the sounds around him. He can hear the different songs of the birds high up in the tree's branches. He can identify them as he listens. A cardinal, a mockingbird, and sparrows are all sharing the tree together. Thinking about the walk with Clay, he remembers the candy store. He can smell the candy canes, chocolates, and caramels. He can see Clay counting out the coins for the candy by feeling the size of each one. A walk with a friend who is blind has given young Jack something new to think about. How life is lived by faith and not by sight.

CHAPTER 6

MEET ABIGAIL ROSE

It's two o'clock on Monday afternoon. Jack has spent the morning mowing the lawn and then had lunch. He took a quick shower, dressed, and went outside. He sat down on the front porch steps to wait for Von. At church on Sunday, Jack introduced Von to his new friend, Clay. They talked a few moments, and Mr. Jones came by. He asked if Clay would like to sit with him and Mrs. Jones during the worship time. "I would like that very much," Clay replied. He laid his left hand on Mr. Jones's right arm and said, "I'm ready." Jack and Von walked behind them through the big sanctuary doors. Von leaned against Jack and said with a whisper, "Isn't Clay handsome and charming?"

"I guess so," Jack said, a little embarrassed. Then Von said, "Oh, Jack, I've got some good news. My cousin Abigail is moving down the street from our house."

"That's great, Von," Jack replied. "When is she coming?"

"She's coming tomorrow, and I want her to meet you," she said. Jack could tell she was excited. "Sure," Jack said. "That will be great."

"I'll bring her sometime after noon, tomorrow," she replied. The choir started singing, and Von said in a hurry, "We better sit down. See you tomorrow." She hurried to the front and sat with her parents.

The porch steps are not very comfortable, so Jack ran for the tree. Up in a flash, he sat back against a big limb and looked up at the sky through the branches. He knows how excited Von is about Abigail's coming. Von has spoken of Abigail many times in the past. Von's and Abigail's mothers are sisters. The sisters were very close growing up. When they married, their husbands' jobs caused them to live in different cities, too far away to see each other except on Thanksgiving and Christmas. It was on those holidays that Von and Abigail decided they wanted to be like sisters.

An airplane way up high has caught Jack's attention. He watched until it disappeared, and then he heard someone calling, "Jack, are you up there?" He recognizes the voice. It is Von. "Coming down," he shouted, and then he lowered himself to the sidewalk.

Von smiled as she pointed and said, "Jack, meet Abigail Rose, my cousin."

"Hi," Jack said as he looked at Abigail. Abigail is ten years old, the same height as Von, with glowing red hair, and freckles across her nose and cheeks. She reached out to shake hands with Jack and said with a giggle, "Call me Abby, Jack. Is Jack short for Jackson or Jackie? Oh, I bet your name is John, and they just call you Jack. Some men are named John, and everyone just calls them Jack. I haven't figured that one out. Is your name really John, Jack?" She took a breath. Jack looked at her a little bewildered and answered, "No, my name is Jack."

"Hmm, strange," she replied and quickly changed the topic. "So this is the tree Von told me about? Is it an elm tree? Wow, it's really tall, isn't it? Did you know there are five species of elm trees, in this state alone? What kind of birds do you have up there? My favorite is the mockingbird. They just sing and chatter and chatter and sing."

"Abby," Von interrupted. Abby looked at Von and said, "Yes, Von." Von is making a zipper motion back and forth across her mouth. Then Von looked at Jack and said, "Abby reads a lot."

"Read a lot, know a lot, I always say," Abby quickly defended herself. Von is making the zipper motion again. "Fine," Abby replied as she rolled her eyes and folded her arms, looking sternly at Von. Von looked sternly. Then both girls laughed. Jack smiled. He doesn't really know what to say. Then Von took each of them by the hand and said, "Let's go to my house. Mother made brownies for us." Jack laughed and said, "Now that's something to talk about. Let's go." Down the sidewalk they went.

Abby began to walk a little faster and asked, "Are they cake or fudge brownies?"

"Oh, I know," she continued speaking with excitement. "They are double chocolate. I hope they have walnuts. Do you like walnuts, Jack? You have got to try them. They are great." Von is giving Abby the zipper sign again. Abby rolled her eyes and replied, "Jack said brownies were something to talk about. I'm just making conversation, Von." A stern look from Von followed. "Fine," Abby sighed. "It's going to be a dull walk, without conversation." Von put her hand over her mouth and giggled. They soon went up the slight hill, and the trio can see Von's house. "Race you," Abby said as she took off. Von and Jack broke into a run across the grass and stopped at the porch. Abby is already sitting on the old porch swing. "Slow pokes," she said, laughing, as she pushed the swing back and forth with one foot.

Von's mother took out a basket of brownies and a pitcher of ice-cold lemonade. Bobby and Ted joined in the refreshment. They talked about school since it will start very soon. Von and Abby are the oldest and will be in the same grade. Von hopes that she and Abby will be in the same class. Bobby and Jack are in the same grade, and Ted is the youngest. Abby leaned back in the swing and said, "Great brownies, but I wished they had walnuts. I'm nuts about walnuts. Oh, I made a funny." She giggled. "Granny Rose always makes brownies with walnuts. Granny Rose bakes a lot of brownies and cakes and pies and cookies."

"Ugh, boy, I'm full," she said, causing the others to laugh. She said with excitement, "Granny always bakes the most at Christmas. It's her favorite time of year. She bakes and bakes, and we eat and eat. Granny calls the family her Christmas roses. Get it?"

"Christmas roses," she said, laughing. "Abby," Von said with that familiar look."

"Fine," Abby replied. "I will talk so you can't hear me." The others laughed. Bobby asked, "How are you going to do that?"

"Watch," replied Abby as she began to make gestures with her fingers and her hands. Jack asked, "What is that?" Von answered, "It

25

is sign language, used to talk with someone who is deaf." Jack walked toward Abby as he watched her do the signs and asked, "How does it work?" Abby explained as she made different signs. "You can make letters with your fingers like this." Then she continued making signs with bigger motions.

"There are also motions that you can make that are whole words or phrases," she said, finishing her demonstration.

Jack is impressed with her work and said, "Abby, that's really something."

"It was my father's idea," Abby replied with a big smile. "Is it because you talk so much?" Bobby asked in a teasing manner.

"No, silly," Abby replied, still smiling. "My father said, an enthusiastic and intelligent girl like me needs a way to channel her energies." Bobby laughed. Jack asked, "Abby, will you teach me to say my name in sign?"

"Me too, Abby," said Von with excitement. "Let the class begin!" shouted Abby.

For the rest of the afternoon, Abby taught, while Jack and Von worked hard to learn the correct signs. After a while, Abby decided it was time to put her students to the test. She had Von and Jack tell each other their name in sign. "Very good, class," Abby said, clapping her hands. "Thanks, Abby," Jack said. "Thank you, sis," Von said, smiling and winking at Abby. Abby hugged Von. "Well, I better go home now," Jack said. "Everybody, remember my birthday party is Friday at two o'clock," he added as he waved goodbye. They all replied, "We'll be there." Bobby and Ted went in the house, and Von walked Abby home. On his way home, Jack can hear the birds singing as he passes the different trees that line the sidewalk. He thought it would be a terrible thing to be unable to hear their songs and all the other wonderful things in the world. His walk downtown with Clay came to mind. He is still amazed at how his blind friend can see by listening, and now Abby tells him, those who are deaf can hear by seeing. He thought to himself, "Clay is right. There is always more to learn."

CHAPTER 7

A BIRTHDAY TO REMEMBER

It's Friday morning, and the Andrews family is at the breakfast table. Jack is excited that his birthday is finally here. His mother has made his favorite waffles, and Mr. Andrews has taken the whole day off work to help get everything ready for the party. As Jack thinks of the people who are coming to the celebration, he thinks of Clay. He asked, "Dad, how long have you known Clay?" "Since we were boys," his father answered. "We grew up together all the way through high school."

"Well, how did you meet him," Jack asked with a curious look.

"I was a lot like you as a boy, Jack," his father began. "There was a big tree that I used to spend time in."

"Really?" Jack replied, even more curious. "Where was the tree?"

"On the other side of town, not far from where I grew up," his father answered. "It is still standing there, big and tall."

"But what about Clay?" Jack asked. His father sat his coffee cup down and began the story. "I was in the tree one day, sitting and looking at my new pocketknife, when I accidently dropped it. I had just started down, when someone said, 'I've got it.' Then the voice said, 'Coming up.' It was Clay. He handed my knife back to me and said, 'What are you doing?' I explained to him that my father had just given me the knife and I was about to carve my initials in the tree when I dropped it. We talked awhile, and then we both carved our initials in the tree. I carved mine JA, and he carved his CS." Jack is smiling as he listens. His elbows are on the table, and his chin is resting on both hands. In his thoughts, he can see the two boys in the tree. He is thinking how good it would be to carve his own initials in the tree out front, where he spends so much time. "After high school, I went to college, and Clay became a navigator in the air force."

"Boy," replied Jack, "a navigator."

"We stayed in touch by letters until Clay's accident." Jack asked with concern, "What happened?" His father explained that, while Clay and his crew were on a training mission, their plane lost power and went down. Most of the crew was injured, and Clay was unconscious for several days. When Clay woke up, his eyesight was gone. "So that's how he became blind," said Jack softly. "Yes," his father replied. "He had other injuries too, and it took months for him to get better." Jack looked up at his father and said, "He's a good man, isn't he, Dad?"

"He certainly is, Jack," answered Mr. Andrews. "Clay is also a man of faith." Mr. Andrews stood up as he finished his coffee and said, "We've got a party to put together, young man. Are you ready?" Jack quickly left his chair and said, "You bet."

Jack and his father worked together on the decorations until noon. "That should do it," said Mr. Andrews. "Lunch is ready, boys," Mrs. Andrews called from the kitchen. "Hungry, son?" Jack's father asked. "You bet," Jack answered. They followed the smell of chocolate cake all the way to the kitchen. "Smells great, Mom," Jack said as he sniffed the air. "I can hardly wait."

Two o'clock finally came, and the excitement is filling the house as friends and neighbors arrive. The little table next to the front door is quickly disappearing under the many gifts they have brought. An hour's worth of games and laughter, everyone is ready for cake and ice cream. Jack's mother began the happy-birthday song, and Abby led with sign language. "Make a wish, Jack," his mother said, thrilled with how things have gone. Jack blew out the candles, and everyone cheered. Mrs. Andrews sliced cake, while Mr. Andrews dished out the ice cream. Jack and Von sat on the hearth of the living-room fireplace. Bobby and Ted sat on the floor and leaned against the stone wall of the fireplace. Abby chose to stand center stage as she ate her cake while sharing bits of knowledge she had gained from her newest book on honeybees. "Oh, they are fascinating," she began. Other conversations are going on in the room. Mr. and Mrs. Andrews and Mr. and Mrs. Jones, along with Clay, are laughing and talking also. "And that's just half of the book," said Abby, realizing she has told all she knows regarding the new book. "When are you going to open your presents, Jack?" she asked as she put the last bite of cake in her mouth. "Yeah," Bobby said, "let's see what you got."

Mrs. Andrews overheard and said, "I think now is a good time. Let's all gather round." Everyone crowded around the table, and Jack began opening all the gifts. He is excited at the gifts his friends have brought for him. "There is a magnifying glass, a baseball bat, a canteen, comic books, and a flashlight. Thanks, everyone," Jack said as he looked around the table. The last gift is a very small box. Jack picked it up, peeled back the bright red paper. "Wow!" he shouted as he held up a beautiful pocketknife. Everyone is excited with him, especially Bobby and Ted. They asked, "Who gave you the knife?" Mr. Andrews answered with enthusiasm, "It is from Clay."

"Happy birthday, my friend," Clay said. "Thank you," Jack responded, still excited. "I love it." He began opening the different blades when Bobby asked, "What's that on the side?" He reached toward the knife and pointed. Jack folded the blades back in place and turned the knife over. Carved deep in the knife handle are the letters JA. "It's got my initials on it. Thank you, Clay," he said, excited. Clay and Mr. Andrews both laughed, pleased at young Jack's excitement over the gift. The children talked about the gifts on the table while the grown-ups clean things up.

Mr. Jones patted Jack on the back and said, "Happy birthday, Jack. We best be getting on home." Mrs. Jones gave Jack a big hug with a tear in her eye. She has known Jack since he was a baby. "Thank you, sir," he replied. "Thank you, Mrs. Jones," he said as she kissed him on the cheek. Von, Bobby, Ted, and Abby all turned as they reached the door and said, "Happy birthday, Jack."

"Thanks, everybody," Jack replied as he waved goodbye. "See you tomorrow." Clay walked forward and put his hand on Jack's shoulder. "Happy birthday, Jack," he said. "Thank you, sir. It's the best." Clay asked if Jack might walk with him on his way home.

Looking up at his father, who nods, Jack answered, "Sure, that would be great."

Clay said good-bye to Jack's parents, and the two friends started down the sidewalk. Jack is still holding the knife. Running his finger up and down the carved initials, he asked, "Did you carve the letters yourself, Clay?" He has learned that Clay is able to do so many things. He can hardly wait to hear how it was done. "The initials were carved by someone else a long time ago," he answered. "The knife was given to me by a very good friend, just before I joined the air force. My friend and I used that knife to carve our initials in a tree the first day we met." Jack is moved by what he heard. "So this is the knife Dad told me about this morning? Grandpa gave it to him, and he gave it to you because you were his friend."

"Wow," he whispered. Clay stopped walking and knelt on the sidewalk. Reaching forward, he placed a hand on each of Jack's shoulders and gently pulled him next to his side. "Jack," he asked, "do you remember the story I told you of my friend who came to me when I became blind and was afraid?" Jack immediately responded," "Sure, I remember. He told you about Jesus being the light of the world." Still holding Jack close, he pointed to the knife in his hand. "My good friend, who gave me the knife, is the same one who told me those things. It is your father, Jack. Now you are my friend too, and I want you to have the knife." Jack's eyes are filled with tears. He is so moved by what he has been told. "Thank you, sir," he said as he wiped his eyes. Clay patted him on the back and said as he stood up, "Enjoy the knife. I'll see you again soon." He opened the little wooden gate that led up the sidewalk to the front door. "See you soon," Jack said as he slowly turned and headed back down the sidewalk that led home.

He looked at the knife as he walked and ran his fingers gently over the initials his father carved so long ago. He carefully placed it in his pocket as he continued the walk home. Not far from home, he started to run. Leaping up on the front porch, he threw the old screen door back and went inside. "Thanks again for the party, Mom," he said as he entered the kitchen. "You're welcome, son," she replied. Then Jack asked, "Dad, will you take me to see the tree you used to climb?"

"Well, I think we have time. Sure, let's go," he said as he kissed Mrs. Andrews on the cheek. "Back in a while, dear," he said as he pulled the car keys off the shelf, next to the back door. "Have fun, boys," she replied as she continued putting away the dishes. They got in the car and started across town. After a few minutes of silence, Jack looked at his father. "Dad," he began, "Clay said you were the one that helped him not be afraid of being blind." His father replied, "I only reminded him that Jesus would help him. Clay had to believe, and Jesus did the helping." Jack answered back, "Still, Dad, I think it was a great thing you did for Clay." His father smiled at him and answered, "We should always help others, son. Remember the golden rule: do unto others, as you would have them do unto you?"

"Sure, I remember," Jack replied, smiling. "Here we are," Mr. Andrews said as he stopped the car beside the road and pointed. "Wow," Jack said as he got out of the car. "Look how big it is."

Approaching the base of the tree, Jack looked up through its branches. "Can I climb it?" he asked. "Sure," his father answered. "I'll give you a boost. Careful now."

"I will," Jack answered as he grabbed the first big limb. Carefully he made his way up the limbs of the tree and found a good place to sit down. He is higher than he has ever climbed before. It is beautiful. Looking up, he sees something but can't quite make out what it is. He reached for the next limb and climbed higher.

There is a place on the tree where the bark has been peeled back. It is smooth and dark. The bark on the edges have grown thicker, making the area look like a picture frame. In the center is the evidence of how a long friendship began. Jack traced over with his finger the initials his father and Clay had carved in the wood so many years ago. "Are you all right, son?" Mr. Andrews called. "Sure," Jack answered. "Down in a minute." He pulled his knife from his pocket. "Don't drop it," he whispered to himself. Leaning against the tree, he carefully carved on the hard wood. Finishing, he blew across his work and ran his fingers over it and smiled. He placed his knife back in his pocket and shouted, "I'm coming down!" With his father's help, he is back on the ground. His father put his arm around Jack's shoulder, and they walked back to the car. Mr. Andrews turned the car around and started down the road home. "Have a good birthday son?" Jack looked at his father with admiration, and said, "The best- ever." He looked back at the tree until it disappeared out of sight. A tree that now has three sets of initials, which read JA for Jack Andrews, CS for Clay Sanders, and JAJ for Jack Andrews Jr.

CHAPTER 8

CR-R-R-A-A-CK

A new school year has begun, and the first six weeks report cards have just been handed out. Jack is walking home as he reviews his grades. *I did all right,* he thought to himself. He placed his card in the middle of the book he is carrying. He looked up at the trees that line the sidewalk. Summer is over, and fall is rushing in. The leaves of the trees have turned from their lush green color to various shades of yellow, red, and gold. There are still plenty of birds in the trees. Their songs are being carried by the cool late-October wind. The leaves are fluttering in the breeze and often break lose and take flight.

His walk has led him home and right in front of his favorite tree. It is taking on a new beauty also. The sun's rays are dancing off the colorful leaves. Setting his book down on the brown grass, he jumped up, caught hold of a limb, and climbed up. He sat down and leaned against the tree's great trunk, as he has done so many times before. He pulled his cap down a little tighter on his head as he looked up through the tree's limbs. It is still his favorite place to spend time alone. *After all, the only thing that has changed are the colors of the leaves, and they are certainly beautiful,* he thought to himself. He reached forward and pulled a big golden-colored leaf from a branch. He brushed it across the side of his face and then placed it in his shirt pocket. The locusts no longer sit and hum in the tree, and the fireflies no longer dance in the evening. Jack knows that soon the leaves will all disappear and the tree will be bare. He sighed. Then excited, he said to himself, "Snow, the snows will come next." That meant snowmen, sledding, snowball fights with Bobby and Ted, and

33

snow angels for Von. Von always loves to make snow angels. The daylight hours are much shorter now, and Jack has already begun some hobbies in his room to occupy himself. He has model airplanes to build and some large puzzles, but for now he is building a kite. It is yellow, and it will have a big red dragon on the front. *I've got to finish before tomorrow,* he thought as he dropped to the sidewalk. Jack's family and the families of Von and Abby have arranged to have a picnic together at a nearby lake. All the children have agreed to bring a kite. "It will be great," Jack said with enthusiasm.

He pulled the screen door back and entered the house. He went to his room and started back to work. He even ate his dinner in his room as he put the finishing touches on the kite. With a big yawn, he pushed his chair away from the desk and looked at the small clock next to his bed. It's ten o'clock, and Jack is worn out. He sat the kite in the corner of the room against the wall, turned out the light, and went to bed.

Saturday morning has arrived. Mrs. Andrews is cooking breakfast and putting the picnic basket together for the day at the lake. Mr. Andrews and Jack are busy making sure all the other things are packed in the car. It is going to be a good-weather day. The wind is blowing, and the skies are mostly clear with high thin clouds. Jack is looking over his kite once more to make sure everything is just right. He took the end of his ball of string and tied it to the front of the kite and gently laid it all on the car's back seat. He has worked long and hard on the kite and is pleased with his work. "Breakfast is ready, boys," Mrs. Andrews called. "Hungry, son?" Mr. Andrews asked. Jack answered, "You bet."

"Let's go get it," his father said as he opened the back door. Jack is so excited about the day ahead. His mother had to ask him twice to slow down and enjoy his food. He responded with a smile as he pulled his fork from his mouth and slowly chewed and then swallowed. "Much better," his mother said, smiling. After breakfast was finished, and the dishes were put away, the Andrews were on their way to the lake.

Jack's mother and father talked casually as his father drove the car. Jack is thinking about all the different things he might do today. He especially wonders how the kite will perform. He hopes he has done a good job on the construction of it. It wasn't a long drive. They are already pulling off the main road onto the winding gravel road that leads to the lake.

Mr. Andrews drove the car up to the parking area that looks slightly downhill at the lake and parked. Looking forward over the front seat, Jack can see the others walking to the grassy picnic area. He opened his car door and grabbed his kite. "Can I go ahead with the others, Mother?" he asked, excitedly. "Go on," she replied. "We will catch up." He took off in a run, holding his kite with both hands. "Wait for me!" he yelled. Bobby pointed at Jack going toward them and yelled out, "Hurry up, slowpoke!" All the kids stop and wait, giggling and waving for Jack to hurry. Catching up to the group, he asked, "What are we going to do first?" Von answered, "Mother said we have to set up our campsite first." Jack nodded and they all made their way down to the park area.

Von's mother and father, along with Abby's parents, have already begun to arrange things on a table. Mr. Rose suggested that Abby and Von spread the blankets out and the boys should collect wood for the fire. "Let's go," said Ted as he took off toward the tall trees that line the shore of the lake. Jack and Bobby follow. The boys worked as fast as they could, each taking as much as they could carry. Setting the wood down in one spot, Ted asked, "Is this enough, Dad?"

"That will do," he replied. "Everyone is free to go play now."

"Let's go to the water," Abby said. Von ran to the water first. Motioning with her hand, she said, "Over here, everybody."

"What for?" Bobby asked. "For a nature photo," she replied. "What is that?" Abby asked. "Come here, and I will show you," Von said as she motioned for the group to gather. Von then positioned them in a row next to each other at the water's edge. "Now," she said, "everyone bend down and look in the water." As they did, they realized what Von was doing. The water is still and is casting a perfect reflection of the group. "Aren't you the clever one," Abby said, smiling. "I should have thought of that." Ted said, "Let's skip rocks."

"Okay," the others replied with enthusiasm. They skipped rocks and laughed and talked until they heard the call for lunch. "Last one is a rotten egg!" shouted Abby as she took off fast as she could. The rest were right behind her.

The campfire is blazing, and all is ready. The children roast hot dogs, and there is fried chicken with all the side dishes. For dessert, there is apple and blueberry pie. The marshmallows are for a last snack before heading home. When it seemed that everyone had eaten all they wanted, Abby said, "Let's go fly our kites." Jack grabbed his kite. All the other children got their kites, and they started down to the open, grassy area.

Jack quickly unrolled his string. The wind has caught his kite, and up it goes higher and higher. The dragon looks great as it flutters in the wind. Next to him, Bobby let his Jolly Roger go. He laughed as he watched the string spin quickly off the spool as the kite raced upward. Then up went Ted's red, white, and blue box kite. Abby and Von are holding their kites, looking at each other, and Abby yelled, "Ready, go." They both release their kite. First, Von's is higher. Then Abby's rises past Von's as though they were in a race. The two kites are going back and forth, reaching higher and higher. Within a few minutes, all five kites are up. They are beautiful, and the children are proud of the display. Jack laid down on the ground. Holding the ball of string in his right hand, he placed his left hand behind his head. Abby's black bat kite seems alive as it goes up and down. Von's yellow-and-blue butterfly is flying so high, you can no longer see its stripes. Everything is going well, and it takes very little work to keep the kites flying high. Jack's eyes are closed as he enjoys the wind on his face. He can smell the wood smoke of the campfires and the water from the lake. He opened one eye. The dragon is still flying high. "We've been flying for two hours," Abby said as she looked at her wristwatch. "Anyone hungry?" she asked as she tugged on her kite string. "I am," said Bobby. Looking toward the family camp, Von said, "You are in luck. Mother is calling us to come in." Von waved back to her mother and said, "We should get our kites down."

Everyone began to slowly reel in the string on their kites. That is, everyone but Jack. His mind is high in the heavens with his dragon. "Hey, Jack, you asleep?" said Ted. Bobby stepped over and softly kicked Jack on the sole of his shoe. Jack rose without a word and began to bring his kite back to the ground. Abby has her kite down first. "Slowpokes." She giggled as she ran for camp. Bobby and Ted have their kites down now and are right behind Abby. The dragon came down as smoothly as it went up. Jack smiled with satisfaction as he finished winding the loose string around the ball and placed it with the kite on the ground. Von's kite has flown higher than anyone's, so it is taking longer to bring it back down. The wind suddenly began to gust. "I'm having trouble, Jack," Von said as her kite darted from side to side, pulling hard against the string. Just as Jack stepped over near Von, the string snapped, right at the ball. "Whoa," said Jack as the kite was carried away by the breeze. "Don't worry," he said. "We'll get it."

"It's headed for the lake," Von said. "I hope it doesn't land in the water." Together they walked the direction the kite was going, but they couldn't keep up. As they started to run to catch up with the kite, it suddenly fell straight down. It fluttered side to side and then gently landed on a tree that stood on the water's edge. Jack and Von stopped and watched as it rested in the tree's branches. "We'll get it," Jack said with a smile of encouragement. Together they walk to the water's edge. The kite seemed to be undamaged. Jack looked up and down the tree's trunk for the best way up. Smiling at Von, he said, "It's not very high, I can get it." He hugged the trunk of the tree and shimmied his way to the first main branch. "No problem," he said, looking down. Von is a little afraid for Jack. Jack pointed at the sight of his father walking toward them. He waved, and his father waved back. He looked down at Von and said, "If I can't get it, Dad will." He started inching his way toward the kite. The kite is still sitting where it landed, and the wind has slowed to a gentle breeze. Jack is high above the water. Finally, he has reached the kite. He slowly pulled it away from the branch, being careful not to tear it. Bringing it near his body, he turned around and looked down at Von and smiled. "Safe and sound," he said. Then suddenly there was a loud, cracking sound, and Jack, still holding the kite, fell into the water.

Looking at the direction of Mr. Andrews, Von yelled, "Help!" Mr. Andrews immediately ran to help his son. Hitting the cool water, Jack turned loose of the kite, and it floated out of sight. He can see the sun shining through the water. With all his might, he is reaching for the surface, but he keeps sinking. His mind is filled with fear as he fights his way to the surface. He feels cold, and his arms are so heavy. The jacket he is wearing is filled with water. He thought, *I can't make it.* He fought even harder, but the surface of the water gets farther and farther away. All at once, in his thoughts, he can see the faces of Von, Mr. Jones, and Clay. He can hear their voices. *His eye is on the sparrow, Jack,* Mr. Jones said. He can hear Clay's voice. *It is faith that gives us the ability and the courage to do the things we should do.* He hears Von. *Don't you pray, Jack?* He remembers how she looked when she asked that question. Feeling the cold and darkness wrapping around him, he cried out in his heart, *God, please help me.* He reached for the surface again, but down he went. At that moment, he saw a man's hand reach into the water, grab him by the shirt, and lift him out of the water. Everything is suddenly bright again as he comes into the open air. Jack is coughing and exhausted. "It's all right, son," said his father as he carried him from the water and sat him on the grass. He coughed a little more and then began to shake. "Are you hurt, son?" his father asked. "No, sir," he replied, shivering, "Just a little cold."

"We will take care of that," his father replied. "We've got a nice big fire going at camp."

Mr. Andrews quickly removed Jack's jacket and began rubbing his arms and hands. Jack coughed. "I'm all right, Dad. Really, I am. I can walk," he said, looking up, the water dripping from his hair. His father took Jack's face in his hands and looked at him very solemnly and said, "I am very proud of you, son." Jack smiled, stood up, and began to walk alongside his father toward the campsite. Von walked close to Jack's side and said to him, "I was never so afraid in all my life." He looked at Von and said with a grin, "Me either. I'm sorry about the kite." Von nudged his shoulder and said, "Oh, silly." About that time, all the others reach them. Mrs. Andrews threw her arms around Jack and said, "Oh, Jack, are you all right?"

"Sure, Mom," he said with a smile, "Just a little cold." The boys began to tease him a little to lighten the mood. "Hey, Jack, was that a swan dive?"

"I give you a five on that one for effort." Abby added, "May I have your autograph?" All the kids, including Jack, giggle. Almost back to the campsite, Jack looked up at his mother and said, "Can we roast the marshmallows now?" She drew him close to her side, smiled, and said, "As many as you want, but we've got to get you dried off."

"Let's go," said Abby. All the kids, including Jack, ran the rest of the way to the campfire.

Once everyone was back at the campsite, Mr. Andrews took Jack to the car. Jack got in the back seat and began removing his wet clothes. His father handed him a change of dry clothes. He looked up at his father, curious, and said, "Whose are these?" His father answered, "They are yours. Your mother knows accidents happen." Jack smiled and said, "Mom is the best."

"Amen," his father replied, smiling. "Still feeling all right?"

"Sure," he answered as he hopped out of the car. "Hey, jungle boy, let's get started!" Bobby yelled, as Jack came near the fire. The time flew by as everyone enjoyed the hot snacks. No one even mentioned Jack's fall, and he was glad.

The sun is going down as the families repack their cars. It has been a full day, and Jack has fallen asleep during the drive home. The events of the day are playing out in his dreams as he rests on the car's back seat. His dragon is beautiful in the sky. He can see the reflection of himself and his friends in the water. He can see Von's butterfly kite floating gently to rest in the tree. He can hear the tree limb crack as it gives way under his feet. He remembers the struggle against the waters that kept pulling him down and the cold darkness that wrapped around him. Even so, a young boy's soul is at peace, for he has experienced for himself what Mr. Jones told him. God is with the sparrow that falls to the earth, and Jack is sure God was with him as he fell into the water, and heard his prayer for help. It was his first prayer for God to help him in his young life, and somewhere between the water and the campfire, he decided there would be many more to come.

CHAPTER 9

FOR THE LOVE OF MADDIE

Seven o'clock on Sunday morning, Jack is awakened by the sun peeking through his bedroom window. Pulling the covers back, he smells coffee brewing in the kitchen. He jumped down from his bed and started dressing himself for Sunday school. "Good morning, Jack," he heard his mother say. Looking up, as he tied his shoe, he smiled and said, "Hi, Mom."

"Breakfast is ready. Are you hungry?"

"You bet," he replied as he finished the bow on his shoelace. He walked over and hugged his mother tight. They went to the kitchen together, where Mr. Andrews is already having his first cup of the brew. "Sleep all right, son?" he asked. Hugging his father around the neck, he answered," "Like a rock."

Mrs. Andrews finished placing the food on the table and sat down. Jack quickly spoke up, "May I say the morning prayer?" His mother and his father look at him, a little surprised. His father said, "You certainly may." They all bow their heads, and Jack offered his prayer of thanks. It was his first public prayer. When he looked up, both of his parents were looking at him, smiling, and then they said, "Amen." Jack picked up his fork and went to work on the stack of pancakes in front of him. He feels energized, and his parents wonder at it. Then he gave them another little surprise when he asked, "Is it okay if I walk to the church a little early?" His father put his fork down and looked at Jack, wondering, as he watched him eating his pancakes in a hurry. He looked over at Mrs. Andrews, smiling, then turned back to Jack and said, "Sure, you can." His mother asked in a curious fashion, "Are you meeting some of the other children?"

"No," he said, trying to chew and swallow his food, "I thought I would sit in the sanctuary awhile before Sunday school." His mother and his father looked at each other once again. Smiling, his father answered, "Sounds like a good thing to do." Jack then picked up his glass of milk and didn't stop drinking until it was all gone. Taking a breath, he said, "Well, see you at church," and then he was out of his chair. "Take your jacket," his mother said as he went through the door and headed down the hallway. "I will" was his reply as he closed the front door.

Jack stopped on the sidewalk and put on his jacket. He stepped over to his favorite tree and looked up through the branches. So many leaves have fallen off. You can see straight up to the top. He pulled his cap tighter on his head and said to himself, "They will grow back." Off he went on his usual route. The wind has a bite to it as it sweeps the leaves across the sidewalk. "Hi, Shasta," he said as he passed by their usual meeting place. Stopping at the end of the block, he looked both ways and then hurried across. The sun is shining brightly off the church building's tall brick walls. He stopped a moment and held his hand a few inches off the wall. He can feel the cool wind blowing on the back of his hand. On the palm of his hand, he can feel the warmth of the sun shining off the brick surface just as Clay had shown him on their walk downtown. He thought, *Clay is right. You could never find the wall if it was snowing.* He followed the sidewalk to the side entrance, and the door is unlocked. He went in, and as he turned the corner, he saw Reverend Perrin in his office. He waved, and the reverend waved back. Reaching the tall sanctuary doors, he leaned against the one on the right and slowly pushed it open. Stepping inside, he let go of the door and walked to the front. The big stained-glass windows are coming alive in the sunlight.

Standing there, admiring their beauty, he heard a voice behind him saying, "Good morning, young man." He turned around, and there is a lovely young woman sitting on the front pew. "Hello," Jack replied. "I'm

Madeline O'Malley, but you can call me Maddie," she said as she smiled. "I'm Jack Andrews," he answered. "Come, Jack, sit with me," Maddie said as she patted on the seat next to her. Madeline O'Malley is twenty-two years old. She has long dark-brown hair with thick curls at her shoulders. She is of slender build and medium height. She is dressed in a white blouse with long sleeves that have beautiful lace cuffs. She has on a green wool skirt that goes down to her shoes. Jack smiled and nodded as he stepped over and sat next to Maddie. She reached over, took his right hand, and said, smiling, "Tell me about yourself, Jack. I'm to be your new Sunday-school teacher."

"You are?" Jack is surprised at the news. Mrs. Miller has been his teacher for two years. "Yes," Maddie began. "Mrs. Miller has to be away for a while. Her husband, poor man, has come down with an illness. The good doctor says it will take a while for him to get over it. They're me aunt and uncle." Jack smiled. He is taken by Maddie's whole manner. A sincere kindness is in her deep blue eyes. She continued to smile even while she spoke. "Oh, you're wondering about the way I talk, aren't you now?" Jack nodded. Leaning a little closer to him, she said, "Well, I was born in Ireland and came to America as a little girl. I'm afraid I forgot to leave the accent there." She laughed softly. "Do you have friends, Jack?"

Jack nodded and told Maddie about Von and her love for butterflies. He told her about Bobby and Ted, Von's younger brothers. He told her about Abigail and how she can make words with her fingers and talk to those who are deaf. Maddie seemed to hang on to his every word. Then he told her about Mr. Jones and about Clay and all the things they had taught him. "It seems you have some fine friends, Jack," Maddie said. "You bet," Jack answered with enthusiasm, "They're great."

"I'll bet you're a good friend too," she replied. Jack shrugged his shoulders softly and said, as he looked up into Maddie's deep-blue eyes, "I try to be."

"I'll bet you do, Jack." She patted him on the hand. "Being a friend is just as important as having one." The sound of people coming into the building is beginning to increase in the hallways. "We best be getting to class," Maddie said. "You go ahead, and I will be along in a few minutes." Jack nodded and started his way to the classroom. The hallway is busy as people talk and greet one another. After a quick drink at the water fountain, Jack entered the classroom. Most of the kids are already there. He sat down between Bobby and Ted. Von and Abby are talking together. The bell is beginning to ring, and the remainder of the twelve students hurried into the classroom. They are sitting in a row of chairs that face a big wooden desk.

Everyone looked up, and the room became silent as Maddie came through the door and gently shut it behind her. She stood in front of the big wooden desk and said, "Good morning, children. My name is Maddie O'Malley, and I'm going to be your teacher in Mrs. Miller's absence."

"My," she said, smiling, her accent very apparent, "don't you look grand this fine morning." The children all respond with a smile. Their response to the beautiful stranger is much like Jack's. Looking at Von, Maddie asked, "And what is your name?"

"My name is Von," she replied, smiling. "I've been told you like butterflies," Maddie said as she turned and winked at Jack. Von nodded. "I love them too," Maddie replied. "Me perfume is honeysuckle. The butterflies love it. They land on me hands and me hair, but it tickles," she said as she wrinkled her nose, pointing at it. All the children laughed. Abby stood up excited and said, "I'm Abigail Rose, Von's cousin."

"A pretty name for a pretty girl it is," answered Maddie. She added, "I love your freckles." Abby is delighted. One by one, the children were all willing to tell Maddie who they were. Reaching behind with both hands and taking hold of the edge of the desk, Maddie began the morning lesson.

She leaned toward the row of children and asked, "Now, what is the greatest of God's commandments? A man came to Jesus one day and asked that very question. Jesus looked at him and said without hesitation, 'The greatest commandment is to love the Lord your God, with all your heart, and all your soul, and all your strength. The second is to love your neighbor, as yourself.' So how do we love God?

"When I was a girl in Ireland, I dreamed of being a dancer in the ballet. I was always practicing and enjoying every minute of it." She raised her hands above her head and slightly stood on her toes. The children giggle. "I would even pretend I was in the ballet on me ice skates. One cold day, I was skating on the frozen stream that ran through our little town. I was spinning and jumping, and the ice broke through, and into the icy water I went. I was so cold and afraid. I couldn't pull myself out. I cried out, 'God, help me.' Exhausted, I looked, and a man was coming to help me, and he pulled me out of the water. He bundled me up best he could and got me home.

"My mother and father sent for the doctor. He was with me all afternoon and through the night. He was worried about me legs because the water was so cold. The next morning, I woke up and was warm, but I could hardly move me leg." She raised her skirt above her shoes, and all the children leaned forward. There is a shiny metal brace on her right leg. "I was never going to be a ballerina, and I was angry," she said as she smiled. "I said, 'God, this is not fair, you know.'" She leaned forward again and asked, "What do you think God's answer was?" She winked and smiled. "'For God so loved the world that he gave his only begotten son, that whosoever believes in him should not perish but have everlasting life.' Then I read where Jesus said, 'No greater love has any man than this, but that he should lay down his life for his friends.' I can't dance, but I can love. There are lots of things all of us can't do, but we can all show love. God gave us love in Jesus, and how we love Him is to love others." The bell to dismiss is ringing, and not a child is moving. Holding her hands out toward them, she said, "Let us pray together." The children quickly got up from their chairs. Von took Maddie's right hand as Abby took her left, and everyone bowed their heads and joined hands. Maddie smiled as she looked over the circle of children about her and said, "I would like to ask me good friend Jack to lead us." Moved by the things he has heard, he nodded and began the second public prayer of the day and of his life. "Thank you, God, for the love you give us. Help us learn to show your love, and thank you for Maddie." Upon saying "Amen," the children, without hesitation, hugged Maddie, who smiled as she wiped the tears from her face and said, "God bless you all."

CHAPTER 10

"TNT"

It's eight o'clock on Monday morning, and Jack is walking up the sidewalk that leads to the tall front steps of his school building. The sun is shining, making the heavy frost sparkle on the ground and the rooftops. He can see Von, Abby, Bobby, and Ted waiting together at the bottom of the steps. The air is cold. The children are all bundled up in their coats, caps, and gloves. As he approaches, he can tell they are talking about something they are excited about. "Hi, everybody," Jack said as he joined his friends. "Hi, Jack," everyone replied. Von said, "Jack, isn't Maddie wonderful?" Jack smiled and nodded. He understood perfectly what Von meant. The very thought of Maddie, with her accent and smile, caused him to just feel good. "I think she's an angel," Abby said. Looking over to his right and pointing, Bobby said, "Hey, look, a new kid." Ted, looking on, said, "Wow, he is big." Von nudged Bobby's arm and said, "Go and say hi, and find out what his name is."

"Oh, all right," Bobby responded.

They all watched as Bobby walked up to the new boy to say hello. They were completely surprised when the new boy made a fist and put it right under Bobby's nose and said something the group couldn't hear. They can see the surprise on Bobby's face as he slowly turned away from the boy and hurried back to the group. Von, questioning her brother, said, "What did you say to him?"

"I said, 'Hi, I'm Bobby. What's your name?' What do you think I said?" he answered, defending himself. "Well, what happened?" she insisted. Bobby, annoyed, said, "He stuck his fist in my face and said,

'TNT.'" Abby jumped in the conversation, saying, "Well, that was mean. What kind of a name is TNT?"

"The kind that spells trouble," Bobby replied. Von, turning to Jack, asked, "What do you think, Jack?" He shrugged his shoulders and answered, "Gosh, I don't know. Maybe he's scared." The first bell is ringing, and the group joined in behind the other kids, including TNT. As they reached the top step and started into the building, Bobby said, "I sure hope he's not in our grade."

Tommy Nelson Turner, now known as TNT, is taller than Jack and his friends. His hair is red and cut into a flat top. He has a muscular build and is a little on the heavy side. He has fiery blue eyes and a freckled complexion. Because of a transfer in his father's work, the family had to move before the holidays. Tommy has been in town only since Saturday. The second bell to begin class is now ringing, and all the students in the classroom, including Jack and Bobby, have taken their seats. They are waiting for Mrs. Lee, their teacher. There is only soft talk being made around the room. Mrs. Lee will enter any minute, and she likes to find the class "quiet and ready to learn." The door is beginning to open. It's Mrs. Lee, and someone is with her. Not only is TNT in Jack and Bobby's grade, but he has also been assigned to their class. Standing in front of the class with Tommy at her side, Mrs. Lee made the introduction. "Oh no," whispered Bobby, who is sitting at the desk directly behind Jack. Jack managed a tiny smile and swallowed hard as he waited for the news. The only empty desk in the room is right beside him. Mrs. Lee completed the introduction, pointed to the desk, and told Tommy that he could take a seat there. Then Mrs. Lee made an announcement that changed everything for Jack. "Jack Andrews," she said, looking in his direction. "We have no lockers available, so I would like for you to share yours with Tommy." Jack managed a smile and nodded as Tommy sat down at the desk next to him. "Good," Mrs. Lee said. "Let's get started in our history books." Everyone opened their books while Mrs. Lee turned to write on the blackboard. Jack opened his book and looked over at Tommy. *He doesn't look so mean,* he thought.

Maybe we can be friends. He can hear Bobby whisper behind him, "I'm glad I'm not you."

It's noon, and the lunch bell is ringing. Jack sighed as he closed his book and laid his pen down. Mrs. Lee dismissed the class, and all the kids started toward the cafeteria. Jack stayed behind, to show Tommy the location of his locker. "Come on, Tommy, I will show you where the locker is," he said. "Okay, shrimp," Tommy answered as he followed. Stopping at the locker, Jack pointed and said, "This is it, number 311." He opened it up and got his lunch sack, and then Tommy hung up his big jacket. "Come on," Jack said. "You can sit with me and my friends." Neither boy said a thing more as they walked to the cafeteria. The room is filled with chatter, and Jack sees Von, Abby, and Bobby sitting at a table together. They are waving to get his attention, and he waves back. Approaching the lunch line, Jack said to Tommy as he pointed, "My friends are over there. You can sit with us when you get through the line." Tommy picked up a tray, started through the line, and never said a word.

Jack went on and joined his friends. As he took a seat, Bobby said, "Boy, I didn't expect to see you in one piece." Von said, "We heard he sits next to you in class and you have to share your locker with him." Jack nodded as he took a bite of his sandwich. "Well, what is he like?" she questioned. Finishing his bite, he swallowed and said, "I don't know."

"What do you mean you don't know?" Abby asked. "He hasn't said anything. I don't think he wants to be friendly," he answered as he took another bite. "Fine with me," Bobby boasted. "Shush," Von said. Jack spoke up, "I invited him to sit with us."

"Well, that was nice," said Abby as Von nodded, agreeing with her. "I guess he didn't accept your invitation," said Bobby, pointing. They all looked, and there sat Tommy on the other side of the room, eating all alone. Abby frowned and said, "Well, that's just rude. Don't you think that's rude?"

"Shush," Von said as she turned her attention to Jack and asked, "What are you going to do, Jack?"

"Try again tomorrow," he answered as he gathered his lunch sack together. Throughout lunchtime, Jack looked across the room at Tommy sitting alone. He doesn't understand why Tommy won't be friends. The bell to end lunch rang, and the friends all got up and started back to class. Bobby walked alongside Jack and said, "Look on the bright side. He didn't beat you up."

The rest of the day was uneventful. It's three thirty in the afternoon and the end of the school day. The classroom doors swung open, and the hallways were filled with the sounds of children talking and laughing. Jack and Tommy met at the locker they share. Without a word, Tommy grabbed his things and turned to leave. Jack shouted above the chatter in the hallway, "See you tomorrow, Tommy." Tommy never responded, and Jack wondered if he didn't hear him or didn't care to. Exiting the big doors of the building, he saw Von and Abby waiting on the sidewalk. Bobby came running up behind him, yelling, "Hey, wait up!" Jack stopped and turned as Bobby joined him. They walked down the steps together and joined Von and Abby. Von asked, "How did the rest of the day go? Did he talk to you?"

"No," Jack replied as he put his cap on his head. "What can we do?" Von asked earnestly. Bobby spoke up. "Leave him alone. Why take a chance on getting punched in the nose?"

"I agree with Bobby," Abby said. "That would hurt."

"What do you think, Jack?" Von asked. Jack stuck both hands in his jacket pockets and started walking down the sidewalk home. The others walked alongside, waiting for an answer. Von caught Jack by the arm and said, "What should we do?" Jack stopped. He can see the sincere care in Von's eyes. It is always there. He looked at Von and the others and said, "I'm going to pray for him." Von smiled and said, relieved, "Yes, that's what we should do."

"I don't know," said Bobby. "Do you think it will work?" Abby asked as she and the others look at Jack. He replied, "God knows Tommy better than we do. He will know what to do." Von was satisfied. She and Abby agreed to pray for Tommy also.

The walk home is a cold one. The November wind is blowing, and the leaves make a rattling sound as they roll over the ground. Jack stopped at his tree and looked up through the branches. All its leaves are gone. "Knew it would happen sooner or later," he said to himself as he ran to get out of the cold. It is toasty warm in the house, and the smell of fresh baked cookies leads him to the kitchen. "Hi, Mom," he said as he sat at the table and picked up one of the warm chocolate-chip cookies on the platter in front of him. As his mother poured him a glass of milk, she asked, "How was your day?"

"Well, we have a new boy in class. He sits next to me," he said, and then sipped his milk. "That sounds nice," she replied. "Not really, he doesn't want to be friends at all," he answered. His mother can see that he is discouraged. "Just keep trying, dear," she said as she offered him another cookie. "Friendship is always worth the effort."

"I will," he replied, smiling, as he bit into the cookie.

Jack went on to his room. He laid across his bed and brought both of his hands behind his head. He can hear the wind beat against his window. He closed his eyes and let his thoughts go. He remembers the summer months and the good times he had in the tree outside. He can recall how it looked with all its beauty. He knows it will be months before it is that way again, and he longs for those times. Then he thought, *Maybe there is something Tommy misses about where he came from. I would sure be sad if I had to move away.* He said in a whisper, "God, I pray that you would help Tommy. Show me what I can do to be his friend. Amen." This was Jack's first prayer asking God to help someone. He smiled as he opened his eyes and looked at the ceiling. He is satisfied. He has prayed the best he knows how and believes God has heard him. He can hardly wait to see what tomorrow will be like.

The next morning, Jack was excited about going to school, but nothing changed. Each day of the week, he tried being a friend to Tommy, but nothing changed. He asked him every day to sit with him and his friends at lunch, but Tommy still sat alone. Each afternoon, Jack prayed for God's help, but nothing seemed to change. Friday afternoon on his walk home, Jack was discouraged. He was sure God heard his prayers for Tommy, but why don't things change?

That night, while Mr. Andrews was reading in front of the fireplace, Jack asked, "Dad, could you show me what the Bible says about praying?"

JACK: A STORY OF A YOUNG BOY'S FAITH

"I sure can," his father answered as he reached over the nearby table and picked up his Bible. Jack sat on the arm of the big recliner as his father turned to the book of Matthew, chapter 7, verses 7 and 8. He read the text as Jack listened. "Ask and it shall be given unto you, seek and you shall find, knock and the door shall be opened unto you; for everyone that asks receives, and he that seeks finds, and to him who knocks the door is opened." Mr. Andrews waited for questions. Jack asked, "How many times should you ask, Dad? How long does it take for God to answer?" His father placed the Bible on the table and pulled Jack close to him. "God can and does answer some prayers immediately. God always answers our prayers. When we pray for other people, it may seem like nothing is changing, but God is answering."

"Why is it like that, Dad?" Jack asked earnestly. "Well, son, God hears us and begins to do what needs to be done in other people's hearts. God hears us, but the people we pray for may not be listening to him. It may take them a while, maybe even a great while, before they begin to understand. Do you remember me trying to encourage Clay to trust the Lord after he became blind?"

"Sure," Jack responded. "Well, it took a while for Clay to do that. I told him all I could and prayed for him. A lot of time went by, but God answered, didn't he?"

"He sure did. Clay is great," Jack said. He is encouraged. "Three things I want you to remember, son," his father said earnestly. "Keep caring, keep believing, and keep praying."

"I will, Dad, thanks," Jack said as he hugged his father.

Sunday morning after breakfast with his parents, Jack is on his way to church. He wants to spend time in the sanctuary alone. It's a cold and windy November morning. Thanksgiving is just a few days away. He walked down the sidewalk and made his turn down the alleyway. Looking ahead, he sees what appears to be smoke coming from off the wood fence. He knows what it is. "Ready, go." He giggled and then took off in a run. He lost again. There is Shasta with her paws over the fence, waiting for him. She is smiling and barking about her victory. Her warm breath looks like smoke in the cold air.

Jack laughed and patted her head and then continued walking. The wind is getting colder, so after looking both ways at the street, he ran and didn't stop until he came to the side door of the church building. He went in and removed his cap and jacket. It is warm and quiet inside. He waved at Reverend Perrin as he passed by his office and went through the tall sanctuary doors. He stopped and looked at the big stained-glass windows for a moment and turned.

There sitting on the front pew is Maddie, with her head bowed. Her hands are together on her lap. Her lips are moving, but Jack can't hear her voice. He quietly took a seat next to Maddie. She reached over and took his hand. "Amen," she said softly. "Good morning, Jack. Here early, aren't you now?" She smiled. Jack nodded and smiled. "Nothing wrong, I hope," she said as she patted his hand. "Well, I came to pray for someone," he answered. "A friend, perhaps," she said. "Well, not exactly," he answered. Jack told Maddie everything that has happened in the past week with Tommy. "I've prayed for him every day, and so have Von and Abby," he said as he looked up at Maddie. "I'm sure you have done a fine job of praying," she replied. "Don't you give up now," she said. "He who asks receives, and whoever seeks finds.'"

"'Whoever knocks, to him the door is opened,'" Jack joined in, smiling. Maddie hugged him tight. She is pleased at what young Jack is beginning to understand. "That's right. God will answer, Jack. Let's pray together for Tommy," she said as she bowed her head and began her petition to God. Jack bowed his head and listened. He is deeply moved at the voice of this lovely lady praying for a young boy she has never met. He wonders how God will answer. Now it is more important than ever. Maddie ended her prayer as the bell for Sunday school started ringing. "Run along to class, Jack," she said. "I'll be there soon." Jack got up from his seat and said, "Thank you, Maddie."

"You bet," she replied with a wink. Jack smiled, turned, and went on his way. Von and Abby are sitting together, and Jack took the only empty seat, beside Von.

Maddie entered the room and stopped in front of the big wooden desk. Smiling, she leaned forward and said, "Good morning, my wee ones." Everyone responded, "Good morning, Maddie." Every child is smiling. Maddie has won their hearts from their first meeting. She opened her Bible and said, "I would like for you all to open your bibles to the book of Matthew, chapter 5 and verse 44." She waited until everyone found the text. She read, "But I say unto you, love your enemies, bless them that curse you, do good to them that hate you, and pray for them which despitefully use you, and persecute you." Holding her Bible against her chest, she then said, "Last week, we talked about the love of God. We love him by loving others also. Today, Jesus is telling us that there are those who won't make it easy for us to love them, but we must anyway. In the verse we just read, Jesus tells us how to do that. We do good things for them, we wish things to be well for them, and we pray for them."

Abby stood up and said, "That is not an easy thing to do." Maddie replied, "No, darling, it's not." Bobby stood up quickly and asked, "If someone won't be your friend, does that mean he is your enemy?" Abby, still standing, added, "He's talking about the new boy in our school, Tommy Turner. He doesn't want to be friends with anyone." Bobby replied, "But we have all tried, honest." Von stood up and said, "We have prayed for him all week." Maddie laid her Bible aside on the big desk and said, "Yes, I have been told about Tommy. It's grand that you are concerned for him and have prayed for him. You have done exactly as Jesus said to do."

"Then why don't things change?" asked Von. Jack stood up and remained quiet. "What is it, Jack?" Maddie asked. He then answered, "My dad told me that, when we pray for others, God hears us, but the ones we pray for may not be listening to God."

"That's right," said Maddie. "Oh, I am so proud of you all. I have an idea that might help Tommy believe we want to be his friend. Let's give him a welcome-home party. This afternoon is our first children's choir practice. We can have it then. I will bring all the goodies to eat, and we can put up some decorations. The only problem is, how do we get him here?" Jack stood and said, "I will ask him to come, but I don't know where he lives."

"I know where he lives," said Abby. Von turned to her with a look of surprise. Looking back at Von, Abby said," "His father works with Daddy. His office is next to Daddy's. They live three blocks from us, and I can ask Daddy to take us there."

"Well now, children. God has been working, hasn't he?" Maddie responded to the news. "So is it a party then?" she asked as she smiled. "Yes," the children all said, excited about the event. "Five o'clock then, children, and we will see God work again. Let us pray together," she said as she held her hands out. The children all gather around her and join hands. Maddie led the class in prayer. The group of friends are more confident than before and are determined to do their part.

Jack, Von, and Bobby met Abby and her parents at the family car after the worship service. Abby has explained to them everything that Maddie and the Sunday-school class want to do for Tommy. Her father is more than happy to drive them to see Tommy. He told the children that Tommy's father has spoken of his and Mrs. Nelson's concern for their son. Tommy has been quiet and withdrawn at home. "Do you think this will help, Daddy?" Abby asked as her father stopped the car in front of the Turner home. "It can't hurt, kitten. Doing good never hurts," he answered. "Come on," he said as he got out of the car. Everyone got out and followed Mr. Rose up the long sidewalk to the front door. "I'm nervous," said Von as Mr. Rose rang the doorbell. "Me too," said Bobby. The door opened, and Mr. Turner is very friendly and asked everyone to come in. Mr. Rose explained to Mr. Turner that the children have met Tommy at school and want to invite him to a party, followed by choir practice, at the church this afternoon. Mr. Turner thanked them and stepped out of the room to get his son.

In just a few moments, Tommy and his father enter the room. The children can tell that Tommy is surprised to see them. Jack spoke up, "Hi, Tommy." Tommy then politely said, "Hello." Jack began, "We are having a party today at church and choir practice after, and we want to invite you to join us." Tommy looked down and didn't respond. Looking up after a few moments, he asked, "Choir practice?"

"Sure," Jack answered. "It's for the Christmas service." Tommy looked at his father, who said, "I think you should go, son." Turning to Jack, Tommy then said, "Sure, I'll come." All the children smiled as Jack shook hands with Tommy and said, "Great, I'll be waiting outside the church for you at five o'clock." Tommy nodded, and Mr. Rose said, "Let's get going." It's going to be a full afternoon. Everyone is excited. They hope this is the beginning to a friendship with Tommy.

Jack entered the house excited. He told his mother and father all that had happened. They are very happy to hear the news and are very proud of all the children for being so dedicated to helping Tommy feel at home. Jack is eating his lunch as fast as he can while talking with his mother and father. He paused for a moment, put his fork down, and said, "Mom, Dad, I just thought of something."

"What is it, son?" his father asked. "I just realized, a lot of people are trying to help Tommy," he said with a smile. "There is Von and Abby and Bobby and me. Mother encouraged me to keep trying, and, Dad, you taught me what the Bible says about prayer. Maddie has been great too. She and I prayed together for him before Sunday school. Abby's father told us where he lived. When we got there, Tommy's father encouraged him to come to the party. It's like you said, Dad. God has been working, and he is using a lot of people. Wow, I can hardly wait." His mother and his father are happy to hear what young Jack has learned. "It's a wonderful thing to be part of God's work," his father said. "You bet," Jack said as he reached for his glass. He took a few quick sips and asked, "Can I go help with the decorations? I told Tommy I would meet him outside the church." His parents told him it was all right, and out the door he went.

The afternoon passed quickly, but everything is ready, and all the children of the class have arrived. Maddie brought cookies, cake, and punch. The children hung decorations on the walls. They even made a big banner that reads, "Welcome, Tommy." Jack is on his way outside to meet Tommy. Maddie and the children are waiting for Tommy to walk through the door. They hope he will be thrilled. Jack has just arrived at the sidewalk, and a car is slowing down and coming to a stop at the curb. It's Tommy. "Hi," Jack said as he approached the car. "Hi, Jack," said Tommy as he closed the car door. Jack is relieved. This is the first time Tommy has called him by name. They entered through the side door, and Jack showed Tommy where to hang his cap and jacket. They walked around the corner and then pushed open the big sanctuary doors and went inside. Tommy immediately looked up at the big stained-glass windows. "They are really beautiful, aren't they?" Jack said, pointing. Tommy turned toward Jack and nodded. He is smiling. "Well, the party is in our classroom," Jack said as he led the way out through the big doors. "It's this way."

Jack is excited, as they walk the long hall to the classroom. Tommy seems relaxed and happy to be there. "Here it is," said Jack as he opened the door. Tommy stepped in, and the first thing he saw was the big banner that reads, "Welcome, Tommy," with all the children and Maddie standing behind it. He immediately turned and ran.

All the children's faces fell. Maddie responded, "Jack, go after him, please." Jack ran down the hallway to catch up with Tommy. He saw the big sanctuary door slowly closing. He pushed on the door and went in. There is Tommy, standing under the big stained-glass window. His back is turned to Jack, and he is looking down. Jack slowly approached him and said, "We didn't mean any harm, Tommy, honest." Tommy turned around. There are tears streaming down his face. He wiped his eyes with the back of his hand and said, "I loved the house we lived in, my room, our backyard, and my friends. I have been angry at my father and mother. Worst of all, I think I have been angry at God too. I didn't want to make new friends, but you and the others have really tried to be friends with me. When I saw the banner, I was ashamed of how I have treated you and the others." He wiped the tears from his eyes again and looked down at the floor. Jack stepped forward, offered his hand, and said, "Friends?" Tommy looked up and smiled. He shook Jack's hand and said, "Thanks, Jack."

"Let's go to the party," Jack said with excitement. Tommy nodded, and the two new friends walked back to the classroom.

The room was quiet as they reached the door. Jack opened it to find everyone standing and waiting. Upon seeing Tommy, everyone clapped, and Tommy smiled. "Who wants cake now?" Maddie asked. All the children cheered, and the party began. Tommy talked to everyone, and he got a warm hug from Maddie. Jack is pleased to see Tommy happy. While eating his cake, he thought back to that cold morning before school. He can see the look on Bobby's face as Tommy stuck his fist up. It is completely different now. During the party, Tommy went to Bobby and offered his hand in friendship. Bobby shook hands with Tommy, and the two talked and laughed together a long time. Jack is glad that he and his friends did not give up. He is convinced that God has answered their prayers for Tommy. He wonders what other things he might see God do.

"It's been a grand party, but it's time to start our practice," Maddie said. A whole hour of eating the treats and talking together seemed to go by much too soon for everyone. Maddie had everyone stand in two lines, six in front and seven behind. When everyone had their sheet music, she called for their attention. Raising her hands, she asked, "Are we ready now?"

"Silent night, holy night, all is calm, all is bright," they began, and everyone is singing. Maddie has tears running down her face as she continues leading the tempo with her hands. She can hardly contain her joy because of what she is hearing from her young choir. Jack and Von look at each other, smiling as they continue to sing. Abby turned and looked at Von. A tear is running down her freckled cheek as she sings. From the midst of the choir is a high and sweet voice that has caught the attention of everyone in the room. The children are looking around as they sing, wondering whose voice has made the wonderful difference. That is, everyone but Tommy. His eyes are closed, and his face is pointed toward heaven as he sings. It is the beauty of his voice that has captured everyone's attention. Without hesitation, the young choir began the second verse. Jack's heart is full. God has answered in the most wonderful way he could have ever imagined.

CHAPTER 11

IT'S SNOWING

The next day was the beginning of a new school week. Only three days of class, and then school would dismiss for the Thanksgiving holiday. Jack and Tommy are becoming good friends. Tommy also looks forward to enjoying lunch every day with Bobby, Von, and Abby. Each of them has shared their families' plans for the holiday. Abby is going to see Granny Rose. Von, Bobby, and Ted are going to spend the holiday with Grandfather and Grandmother Martin. Tommy is also going away to see his grandparents. Jack is staying home. His grandparents are coming to his house this year. He can hardly wait to tell them of all his new friends.

Everyone had a great holiday, and Jack is glad to see his friends again. The first day back to school, Abby brought some of Granny Rose's chocolate brownies for everyone. Tommy is right at home with his new friends and agrees with Abby. Brownies are much better with walnuts, and Granny Rose's brownies are the best he has ever had. The group of friends is very excited about the Christmas service, especially since Tommy has joined the choir.

Jack and his friends have been very busy with their schoolwork and practicing the songs with Maddie. Maddie and the children's class have made plans for a class Christmas party and will exchange gifts. Colorful decorations of the season are seen everywhere at the stores, homes, and the trees that line the sidewalks. The spirit of Christmas is back once more.

It is now seven days until Christmas, and Jack is on his way home from school. It's Friday, and he is looking forward to helping his father put up the Christmas decorations. It has been a bitter, cold day. The clouds are thick and dark. While Jack had his breakfast, he heard the weatherman say there was a good chance for snow tonight. "Boy, I hope it does snow," he said as he studied the sky. He stopped by his tree and wondered how it would look with snow in its branches. *I need to get my sled ready,* he thought to himself. Pulling his cap down a little, he then ran around to the garage. Opening the side door, he sat his things down and looked up along the back wall. There it is, and Jack is excited as he looks for the ladder. He found the ladder, stood on it, and pulled the sled from the nails it hung on. It is plenty dusty. *I bet I can go even faster this year,* he thought as he ran his hand over the runners. He sat it down and went into the house. "Hi, Mom," he said as he took off his cap and jacket. "Hello, dear. Have a good day? How about some hot chocolate?" she asked with a cup in her hand. "You bet. Thanks, Mom," he answered as he sat down at the table. "Your father should be here anytime now," she said as she sat the cup of chocolate in front of him. "I'll be ready," he answered as he sipped. "I've got to get my sled cleaned up too."

"I hope the weatherman is right about the snow for tonight," he said as he took another sip. His mother is looking out the kitchen window, washing dishes as they talk. She placed the dish she has washed down in the sink, leaned forward, and pulled the window's curtain back to get a better look outside. She sees something. Smiling, she said, "I believe he is right. Look." Jack jumped up and opened the back door. It is snowing. The flakes are gently floating to the ground. "Oh boy, this is great," Jack said, excited. Mr. Andrews entered the kitchen and said, "We better get those decorations up, son."

"You bet," Jack responded. "I just need to change my clothes."

Jack and his father went to the garage and found all the boxes of lights and other decorations and placed them on the grass in the front yard. The snow is beginning to cover the grass, as Jack and his father work fast as they can. Finally, the decorating is done, and it is beautiful. They even wrapped the big trunk of Jack's favorite tree with lights. They went in the garage and put away the tools. "Want some help cleaning up your sled, son?" Mr. Andrews asked. "Sure, that would be great, Dad," Jack answered. Father and son went to work cleaning and polishing. It wasn't long, and they had the sled looking like new again. "Thanks, Dad," Jack said as he joined his father at the garage door. "You're welcome, son," he answered. They walked around to the front yard for a last look at their work. As they admired the display, the snowfall suddenly increased, and Jack shouted with joy. "Looks like you're going to need that sled tomorrow, son," his father said. "You bet," Jack answered. The rest of the evening, Jack looked out the window every few minutes. He is so excited, he feels he can't sleep. He laid on his bed in the dark and tried to imagine the fun he and his friends would have together. The first thing they always do is build a snowman. Von always makes snow angels. Jack wants to take his sled up to the highest hill at the park and see how fast he can go. He took one last look and yawned. It is still snowing, and Jack went to sleep.

It is Saturday morning, and the snow has continued through the night. Jack is beginning to wake up. Rolling over on his back, he closed his eyes again as his thoughts began to stir. He is imagining himself going down a steep hill on his sled. He can almost feel the chill of the snow on his face as he laid in his warm bed. "The snow," he said to himself. Kicking the covers off his feet, he ran to the window and looked out. "Oh boy," he said to himself as he ran to the front door, opened it, and stepped out on the porch. Six inches of new snow covers the yard, and Jack's favorite tree has snow standing all along the branches. It is a beautiful sight. He watched the big flakes float gently to the ground a few moments, then he went inside to get himself dressed. It is early morning and still dark outside, but Jack is ready to enjoy the snow. The Andrews family had breakfast together, as Jack told his mother and father about all the things he wanted to do today. They know he is excited. Once breakfast was over, Jack went to the garage to get his sled. Grabbing hold of the rope tied to the front of it, he laid it over his shoulder and pulled the sled behind him. He is on his way to the Martin house to meet with his friends.

The snow has covered the sidewalk, and the trees alongside it are beautiful, with the snow hanging in the branches. The wind is calm, and Jack can hear the snow crunch under his boots as he walks. He stopped and looked behind him. There are his footprints deep in the snow, with his sled tracks following behind. Jack smiled. He is the first one in the neighborhood to enjoy the first snowfall.

Reaching the top of the hill, he can see Bobby and Ted in their front yard. They are throwing snowballs at each other. "Hi, guys!" Jack shouted as he tugged at the rope of his sled. "Hey, Jack, come on, you are on my side!" shouted Ted. Just as Jack got within range of the two boys, a snowball hit him in the face. "You lose!" yelled Bobby. Jack dropped the rope to his sled and wiped the snow from his face. He reached down and picked up a handful of snow and squeezed it tight with both hands. The snowball fight is on, and it's every man for himself. The boys made and threw as many snowballs as they could at whomever they could. Exhausted, they laid down on the snow to catch their breath. As Jack laid on his back in the snow, he closed his eyes and began moving his arms and legs to make a snow angel. Hearing something, he opened his eyes just in time to see Abby's snowball coming down. "Got you." She giggled. "Hi, Jack," Von said as she laid on the snow and made a snow angel. "Hi," Jack replied, wiping the snow out of his hair and putting his cap back on his head. "Let's build a snowman," Ted said. Everyone agreed and got busy. Even though the snowman leans a bit to the left, the boys are satisfied with the fat gentleman. It became clear that Abby is quite an artist. She made a whole family of penguins out of the snow. Von loves them. "Let's go sledding," Bobby said. Without a word, Jack grabbed the rope to his sled and was ready to go. He has dreamed of this day since October. Bobby and Ted grabbed their sleds, and the group of friends was on its way to the park area. Tommy is going to meet them there.

It is still snowing as Jack and his friends arrive at the park. Tommy is standing on the hill and is waving at them. They all waved back as they continued the walk to join him. Reaching the top, they see a set of tracks that go all the way to the bottom of the hill. Tommy made a trial run while he waited for his friends. "How was it?" Jack asked, excited. "It was great," Tommy replied. The boys decide to have a race on the first run. They all lined up and said they were ready. "Go!" shouted Abby, and off they went. Jack pushed with all his might and laid down on his sled. "Look at him go," he heard Ted's voice behind him. He can't help smiling all the way down the hill. The ride, with the air on his face as he races on the cold white surface, is thrilling. His sled has finally stopped, and he is the first one to the bottom of the hill. Bobby came down second, then Tommy, and Ted finished last. "I'll win the next one," Ted said as he picked up his sled. They made four more runs, and Jack went farther and faster each time.

The group sat down together to rest under a big oak tree that stood on top of the hill. "I'm hungry," Abby said as she pulled her hat down on her head. The wind is beginning to blow. "I'm cold," Ted said. "I'm going home." Bobby agreed the cold wind made it too uncomfortable to enjoy being outside any longer. He decided to go home with his brother. "Tell Mother we will be home soon," Von said as the boys walked away. "We will," Bobby replied. Suddenly the snow began coming down so fast the children could hardly see Bobby and Ted walking down the hill. "Maybe we should all go home," Von said as she stood up from her seat under the tree. "The weather may be getting worse."

"Besides, it is past lunchtime," Abby added. Tommy nodded and said, "It is getting much colder, What do you think, Jack?"

"Sure, that's fine, but can I take one more run before we leave?"

"Be careful, Jack," Von said. "The snow is really coming down fast."

"Don't worry," he said as he placed his sled at the starting point. "Here I go," he said as he pushed hard and laid down on the sled. "Wow!" he yelled as he disappeared into the falling snow. Faster and faster he went, and then he was lifted off the ground. "This is great!" he shouted as he tightened his grip on the sled. Suddenly the sled hit the ground hard, and Jack and his sled separate. He can see nothing but snow as he tumbles and slides to a stop. *Oh, that hurts,* he thought as he pulled himself out of the snow and looked for his cap.

He bent down, put his cap on his head, and brought his left arm gently to his side. "Are you all right, Jack!" shouted Tommy as he and the girls ran to catch up. Jack sat down to wait for his friends.

When Tommy, Von, and Abby reached Jack, they knew something was wrong. "Are you hurt, Jack?" Von asked as she knelt on the snow in front of him. "It is my arm," he answered. "It really hurts." Tommy knelt down in front of Jack and asked, "Can you move your fingers?"

"I can, but it really hurts," he answered. "Abby," Tommy said as he looked up. "May I have your scarf to use as a sling?" Quickly pulling the scarf off her neck, she asked, "Is it broken?"

"It could be, but we need to keep it as still as possible until we get him home," he answered. Tommy took the scarf and made a sling for Jack's arm and helped him stand up. "Thanks, Tommy, that feels better," Jack said as he looked at the sling. "Where did you learn to do that?" Von asked. "You are certainly full of surprises," said Abby as they started for home. "My mother is a nurse," Tommy answered. "She has taught me a lot about first aid." The snow continued to come down as Jack and his friends walked back to the Martin home. Once they arrived, Mr. Martin called for Jack's parents. "Thanks, everybody," Jack said as he got in the car. Mrs. Andrews hugged Tommy and kissed him on the cheek before she got in the car with Jack. He is on his way to the emergency room. His friends hope it is not a serious injury.

CHAPTER 12

MERRY CHRISTMAS

It is Sunday morning. Jack has been sleeping in the recliner that sits in front of the fireplace. Opening one eye, he watched as the red and orange flames danced among the logs. Closing his eye, he nodded off again. His thoughts are taking him back to the hill with his sled. The snow is deep, and the wind is cold. He is going so fast. "I'm flying," he squealed, and then, "Ouch." He opened both of his eyes, but they feel so heavy, so he closed them again. Jack's left arm has a clean break, and it had to be put in a hard cast. The pain medicine he was given is making it hard to wake up. "Six weeks," the doctor said. "Then he will be good as new." Jack reached over slowly as he tried to wake up and tapped the cast with his fingers and sighed. Watching the fire in front of him, he lifted his head. He sees the display of Christmas cards his mother has arranged all along the mantle. There are tall ones, short ones, cards of silver, gold, and red. Jack fell asleep once more.

He has no idea how much time has gone by, when he is awakened by a kiss from his mother. "Want some hot chocolate?" she asked as she ran her fingers through his tangled hair. "You bet," he whispered as he closed his eyes. He is awakened again by the smell of hot chocolate from the cup his mother is holding next to him. He sighed and sat up as best he could. "Thanks, Mom," he said as he managed a smile. He took a sip. It is so good. Feeling better, he sat back and looked at the Christmas cards again. *They are beautiful,* he thought as he got out of the chair and stood in front of the fireplace. "Merry Christmas," the first one read. "Season's greetings," read the next one. All of them from friends and family. One card has caught his eye. It is a picture of Jesus. He has a lamb on his shoulders as he walks, and he is smiling. He read the words under it, "For unto you, is born this day in the city of David, a savior, which is Christ the Lord." Something about the picture and the words has his attention. He sat his cup down on the table and laid back down in the chair as he studied the card, and his heavy eyelids closed again.

Jack slept through the morning and into the afternoon. As he awoke, he yawned and stretched. His body is so sore from his tumble in the snow. He laid his head back against the chair and looked up again at the Christmas card display on the mantle. "I missed Sunday school and church today." He sighed. He missed seeing Maddie and all his friends. His arm hurts a little, and he looked down at it. There is something different about it. Jack had visitors while he slept, and the evidence is written on his cast. "God bless you," wrote Rev. Perrin. "We love you, Jack," wrote Mr. and Mrs. Jones. One especially caught his attention as he gently rubbed his finger over the words. "Get well, my good friend. Love, Clay."

"The man is amazing," he said to himself. Maddie and his friends had also come to visit as he slept. "Glad you didn't crack your head." It was signed Bobby and Ted. Jack couldn't help but giggle. "Praying for you," wrote Von. Abby wrote "Love ya" in artistic big letters. "Feel better soon," Tommy wrote. He has become very special to Jack. All the other kids from his class had also signed their best wishes. Tears welled up in his eyes as he read the note written just below his fingers. "With all my love, Maddie."

Jack is feeling much better this evening. He had a good dinner and even got to bathe and change his clothes. He has been looking out the living room window for the last few minutes. The snow has stopped earlier today, leaving eight inches of the sparkling white powder. As he left the window, the Christmas card, showing Jesus carrying the lamb, caught his attention once more. He went to the mantle and picked up the card and sat down in the recliner. He studied the beautiful picture a moment and read the scripture reference again. He turned to his right, where his father is sitting on the sofa, reading. "Dad," he said as he held the card up. "Will you tell me the meaning of this card?" His father nodded as he sat down next to him and took the card from his hand. "What would you like to know first, son?" he asked. "Well, I know we celebrate Jesus's birth on Christmas, but I'm not sure I understand the word *savior*. What does the lamb on his shoulders mean?"

"Those are very good questions, son, and I'm glad you asked," his father replied as he reached for his Bible.

"The card is reminding us of a parable that Jesus told of the ninety and nine," Mr. Andrews said as he turned the pages of scripture. He stopped at Luke, chapter 15, verses 1 through 9. Jack and his father read them together. Mr. Andrews began his explanation. "Son, there are certain laws, or forces, that are set in motion in the world we live in. Some of those are physical, and some are spiritual. Yesterday, you experienced the effects of one of the physical laws." Jack looked up at his father, a little puzzled. "Do you remember studying about gravity in school?" his father asked. Smiling, Jack answered, "Sure, what goes up must come down."

"Oh yeah, my crash on the sled," he said as he patted his cast with his right hand. "That is right," his father answered. "Once you left the ground, you were helpless to defend yourself against that law. There is a spiritual law we are told of in the Bible that we are helpless to defend ourselves against from the moment we are born. It is called the law of sin and death. The Bible says, 'The soul that sins, it shall die,' and 'All have sinned, and come short of the glory of God.'"

"It sounds bad," Jack said with concern. "It is, without Jesus," his father answered. "Son, when Jesus died on the cross, he was paying the price of our sin with his own life. When Jesus rose from the dead, it meant he was greater than sin because he defeated sin. Jesus said, 'I am the resurrection and the life.' He also said, 'Because I live, you shall live also.' He said that before he went to the cross, because he is the Savior.

"The lamb that Jesus has on his shoulders represents those who have believed on Jesus and have been saved by him. Remember what we just read from the scriptures? Jesus said, 'What man of you, having a hundred sheep, if he lose one of them, does he not leave the ninety-nine in the wilderness, and go after that which is lost, until he finds it?' Remember Zacchaeus?"

"Sure," Jack replied. "I always wondered how Jesus knew he was in the tree. Is it because he was looking for him?"

"It is, son. Jesus called himself the good shepherd, who would lay down his life for the sheep. He also said that the shepherd, knows his sheep by name, and the sheep know his voice and follow him." Jack was quiet for a few moments. He looked up at his father and said, "So all of us are the lost sheep."

"That's exactly right, son," his father answered. "Jesus became my savior when I was your age." "What about Mom," Jack asked. "Your mother was twelve when she asked Jesus to be her savior."

"I believe in Jesus, Dad," Jack said as he placed the Christmas card on the fireplace mantle. "So all I have to do is ask for Jesus to be my savior?" His father opened his Bible once more and stopped at the book of Revelations, chapter 3, verse 20. Then he said, "Let's read it together, son." They read, "Behold, I stand at the door and knock: if any man will hear my voice, and open the door, I will come in to him, and I will have fellowship with him, and he with me."

"You are right, son," his father said as he closed the book. "The door is your heart. All you need to do, is ask. I want you to do something for me, son."

"Sure, Dad," Jack answered with a curious look. "I want you to think about these things for a while, and if you have any questions, I want you to come to me."

"Sure, Dad, I will, thanks."

"Your mother and I will be praying for you," Mr. Andrews said as he placed the Bible on the table. "I know," Jack replied with a grin. "I heard you one night. It really means a lot."

Jack spent the next few days in the house. The snow was still deep on the ground, and he still had pain in his injured arm. During the day, he helped his mother with the holiday baking. He even learned to crack an egg with one hand. "Wait till Abby sees this," he said as he laughed. In the evening, Jack and his father sat in front of the fireplace and enjoyed talks together.

It is Thursday, and Jack's arm is better, and so is the weather. It's a partly sunny day, and the snow is melting. Jack is enjoying his first venture outside since his accident on his sled. Sparrows are scattered in small groups along the sidewalk, taking baths in the puddles as the snow melts off the trees. "It's so good to be outside," he said to himself as he walked. All the snowmen in the neighborhood are showing the effects of the warmer weather. Jack is wondering how the old fellow he and his friends built is doing. Topping the hill, he stopped in front of the Martin house. There doesn't appear to be anyone at home. The snowman that Jack, Bobby, and Ted had made is leaning even more than before, and the carrot they used for his nose has fallen to the ground. Abby's snow penguins are small mounds of slush. "Oh well," Jack sighed. "Maybe it will snow again soon." He continued walking until he had reached the big hill he sledded down less than a week ago. He stood under the big tree on top of the hill and looked down its slope. He remembers everything about that last ride. It was thrilling, but the cost of falling had come with the ride. Jack has done as his father asked. He has thought much about having Jesus as his savior. Leaning back against the tree, he looked up into the sky for a few moments. Smiling, he knelt on the melting snow to pray. "Dear Jesus," he began as he removed his cap, "I believe you are the savior, and I ask that you would please be my savior, for always, amen." Standing up, he took another look down the long slope and sighed as he smiled. It is done, and even though Jack is ten years old, he somehow feels brand-new. There is one thing left to do.

He put his cap on his head and whispered, "Thank you, God." Down the hill he went. His mind determined and his heart full, Jack didn't stop walking until he was in front of Community Church. He walked down to the side door as he has so many times before and went in. He removed his cap and unzipped his jacket as he rounded the corner of the hall. Reverend Perrin is in his office. He waved at Jack through the window. Jack waved back, only this time, he opened the door to Reverend Perrin's office and went inside.

It's Christmas Eve, and it has been a day filled with activity. Jack, his mother, and his father are in the car together, on their way to the church building. Jack is wearing his angel costume, and his cast isn't visible at all. He is filled with anticipation as they pull into the parking lot. While the children's choir sings, there will be others dressed in costume as they tell the story of that night in Bethlehem. Jack has already told his parents of his prayer on the hill, and they are thankful to God and very proud of their son. The hallway is busy, as those in costume make final preparations. The sanctuary is filled with people eagerly waiting to begin. Jack hurried off behind the stage curtain and took his place in the choir beside Von. She gave a nervous smile and squeezed Jack's hand as the curtain went up.

Maddie called the choir to attention. "All right, me angels, let us sing."

"Silent night, holy night, all is calm, all is bright," they sang. Jack can see his mother and his father sitting on the front row. Mr. and Mrs. Jones are sitting behind them. Everyone in the audience is smiling. As they finished the last verse, a single light, beaming downward, revealed the manger, just below the stage. Tommy sang, "O little town of Bethlehem, how still we see thee lie." His high, sweet voice promoted a sense of reverence as Mary and Joseph walked down the aisle and took their place at the manger. The shepherds are making their way to the manger now, and Jack's heart is welling up with joy as he watches them approach and kneel. "It came upon a midnight clear," the young choir sang as the wise men slowly approached the manger scene. There are three of them, and Jack's heart is pounding with joy as he recognizes the first wise man. It is his good friend Clay.

Now is the finale. Everyone in the audience stood, and joined in, as the young choir sang, "Joy to the world, the Lord is come." Upon the last notes, the audience clapped, and all the lights of the sanctuary were turned on. Maddie expressed her joy by blowing a kiss toward the young singers. Reverend Perrin approached the front of the stage, and asked everyone in the audience to be seated. He thanked Maddie and her choir for the beautiful songs. He then thanked all the cast for their participation in the celebration of the birth of the savior. Jack is a little nervous as he waits for Reverend Perrin's next words. "There will be a baptismal service this Sunday," the reverend said with a smile. "We are going to baptize young Jack Andrews." Jack saw his mother's tears of joy as his father hugged her close. Von and Abby hugged Jack tight. "Amen," he heard a loud voice say. It was Mr. Jones. Maddie blew another kiss, and called Jack's name. She smiled and cried. His heart is pounding as he looks around at the joy expressed by everyone. It is truly a merry Christmas. Looking around, he sees so many faces, of those who have touched his young life, and he is grateful. So much has happened, and he has learned so much. Soon, a new year will begin. Jack can hardly wait to see what will take place, and as someone who knows Jack very well, I can hardly wait myself.

ABOUT THE AUTHOR

Jack Crockett grew up in the small town of Howe, Texas. He went to Christ at the age of nineteen and surrendered to the ministry a year later. While working in a skilled trade, he has pastored small churches in North Central Texas and has taught the Word of God throughout his life. He is a resident of Whitesboro, Texas, with his wife, Vonnie. They have two grown daughters and six grandchildren. This book is Jack's first published work.